This is the book I would most like to give  aspiring independent directors but to exe The book provides assurance that the skill can be learnt.

By building core capabilities and learning how to deploy those wisely you can find your voice, be heard in a way that is true to who you are and be effective. So, I found the book wonderfully practical, refreshingly clear and straightforward, and just helpful. I would have liked someone to have given my younger self something like this with encouragement to practise! Like any muscle, it gets stronger the more you use it. That said, it also made me think about how I behave currently so that we can all learn something new.

Tracey Killen, Former John Lewis Partnership Main Board Director and Portfolio Non-Executive Director

This is a very valuable book with practical tools to both help individual board members and boards prompt challenging topics of conversations, and rise to the growing challenges to organizations in a new era where purpose, sustainability and inclusion need to be central.

Bevis Watts, Chief Executive Officer, Triodos Bank

This is the book I wish I had read at the start of my NED career – however, even after some years in the role, it has given me a huge amount of valuable advice and guidance, which I will definitely make use of in my current positions.

Board Talk is a highly readable book, which provides an engaging and relevant approach to the way board members can be most effective in their role and bring real value to their boards. In many board meetings, there is often a limited time for each NED to make a contribution; the advice in this book will help to ensure that all interactions, both in and out of formal meetings, can be as meaningful and relevant as possible. I thoroughly recommend it, whether you are a new or experienced board member.

Mary Champion, Portfolio Non-Executive Director
and Board Member

Board Talk is an indispensable guide for board members seeking to navigate today's complexity and constant change. With its comprehensive coverage of 18 crucial conversations, this book equips readers with the tools to foster effective dialogue inside and outside the boardroom. The authors' expertise shines through as they address key topics such as strategy, accountability and working relationships. Whether you're a seasoned board member or aspiring to join a board, this book offers invaluable insights and practical advice.

Berrak Banu Kurt, SVP and Head of People and
Culture, Volvo Group

In my experience, boards work best when members of the board can communicate clearly with each other. It is all too easy to become buried under mountains of papers, presentations, accounts, risks registers and performance charts. All of these things are necessary but the real power of a board is when we can talk and engage executives and non-executives together. Each brings a different perspective through their own knowledge and skills. Our best boards are inclusive and diverse. They are open, transparent and courageous. To be that and deliver that, we need to have conversations that seek to clarify, challenge, support and inspire. This book sets out the journeys boards need to be on. The authors take us through 18 conversations that populate what makes a great board.

Professor Steven West, CBE, DL, FRCPodM, FRSM,FRSA,
honMFPH, Vice-Chancellor, University of the West of England

A wise, accessible and energizing book and an invaluable handbook for board chairs and members at all levels, and those aspiring to board roles.

Dame Shan Morgan, NHS Foundation Trust Chair

This book shines a light on what actually happens in a boardroom – not just the formal processes of corporate governance, but how board members interact, what they need to know and how they can make effective contributions. Essential reading for anyone on a board, or who would like to step up to the board.

Colin Skellett, Group Chief Executive, Wessex Water

This is an authoritative, accessible and practical book that will help board members get beneath the governance codes to see and understand what's really going on in their boardroom. Underpinned by a well-researched evidence base and a wealth of experience, the book covers the key conversations that boards must have to be effective.

Alison Johns, Chief Executive, Advance HE

This book will be a great source of insight for those taking on board positions or aspiring to do so. I wish it had been available to me at that point in my career – it would have saved a lot of learning on the job.

Mike Cartwright, Portfolio Finance Director and CFO

Essential reading for NEDs who want to thrive in the boardroom. This book combines practical, easy-to-read guidance with robust models and techniques. It is not just the book I wish I'd had when I started my non-executive career, it's also the book I'll return to again and again.

Susan Young, Non-Executive Director and Executive Coach

This book is a refreshing look at the importance of communication in making boards truly effective. As an experienced non-executive director, I found some new perspectives to develop my practice.

Gail Bragg, Portfolio Non-Executive Director

KATHRYN BISHOP AND GILLIAN CAMM

Board

Talk

18 crucial conversations that count inside and outside the boardroom

First published in Great Britain by Practical Inspiration Publishing, 2023

ISBN   9781788604147   (print)
          9781788604161   (epub)
          9781788604154   (mobi)

Want to bulk-buy copies of this book for your team and colleagues? We can customize the content and co-brand *Board Talk* to suit your business's needs.

Please email info@practicalinspiration.com for more details.

Practical Inspiration Publishing

MIX
Paper | Supporting responsible forestry
FSC   FSC® C013604

This book is written for everyone who serves on a board, or aspires to board membership – and to encourage those who are thinking about a board role.

Contents

Preface:
Why you need this
book and how to use it

'Businesses, in fact, run on conversations'
Veenman and Cannon (2014, p.29)

Who this book is for

The proposition in this book is that conversation drives good governance in boardrooms in every sector, so if you serve on a board of an organization – or are applying for a board role – this book is for you.

You may be an experienced board member in a public limited company (plc) looking to navigate the changing board context, or a newly appointed board member wondering whether the work of the boardroom is really for you. You may be a senior executive stepping up to the board for the first time, or you may be a trustee of a charity, a non-executive director (NED) of a company, a member of a public sector board or a school or university governor. Although these organizations are, of course, different in structure and purpose, board members in these different contexts have something in common: they share the need to engage in constructive and collective conversations to discharge their duties properly and to add value to the organizations they serve and oversee.

This book will be particularly useful for those we might collectively describe as 'independent board members', namely those who:

- are not involved in day-to-day management but rather in policy and strategy;

- are responsible for monitoring executives and fulfilling the organization's purpose;
- should be taking a longer-term stewardship perspective.

And it may also be useful for regulators and inspection bodies, in looking at the way board conversations and interactions contribute to good governance.

Why you need this book

Board members will want to know whether their board is effective and, if it's not, how to make it better. When we try to answer those questions, we often focus on the structures and processes – quality of papers, terms of reference and schedules of delegations, for example. However, boards need to avoid 'dead rat governance': like the dissected rat in the biology lab, the structures may be there, beautifully interconnected, but the rat is dead. Nothing is happening.

Conversation is what makes the machinery of governance actually work.

There are many excellent books which explain legal and operational frameworks for good governance, and if you are a new board member, they will be useful to you. Governance is intended to ensure and assure the proper use of resources in an organization to achieve its defined ends. So, structures and processes are a part of that, of course – who sits at the board table and how often they meet, what the agenda covers and whether board papers are useful. But no amount of carefully designed process can compensate for a dysfunctional board with members who don't get on, or can't agree, and whose meetings are really a series of speeches rather than constructive conversations.

This book puts the emphasis back on conversations in boards: how they talk to each other and to stakeholders, and what they talk about. This is the means by which boards do their work – understanding information, making wise decisions, overseeing operations, setting the tone from the top, leading. Conversations about the right topics which happen in the right way. Conversations in which there is both talking and listening, where there is questioning, debating, disagreeing and then reaching a workable consensus.

These are not 'soft skills' but human skills, and they matter hugely. Even if board members have insights to offer, delivering them in the wrong way diminishes their value. The monologue about how a non-executive did something in their previous role as an executive rarely lands well – even if the nugget of wisdom in it would be useful. Expressing a key idea in language that is unusual for a particular board may mean that it won't be heard. If a contribution from a director is seen as excessively challenging, or too colourful and emotional, its impact is wasted. Worse still, board members may fall into a pattern of expressing useful ideas in ways that aren't well received. And then their colleagues' ears close as a particular person starts to speak and the board misses the opportunity to hear a perspective that could be significant. Alternatively, there could be the opposite problem: uncertainty or peer pressure prevents an independent board member from saying something that could be pivotal in the conversation.

So, in contributing to their collective work, board members need to think about what they have to say, whether to say it and how they say it. This is not about presentation skills – better, clearer monologues – but about conversation. The interactive listening-and-talking dance which is so important.

How to use this book

This book is not an instruction manual telling you what to do. Neither is it a reference book outlining the latest thinking on boardroom issues such as sustainability or diversity. Rather, it is a book to help you reflect on the nature of your board and your role in it, and to develop better conversations which will help you to perform your role well.

If you are a new board member, you will obviously also want to read the relevant codes, regulations and legislative rules to help you to understand the way your particular board is structured and *what* it does – and you will find other useful material listed in the Appendix. Whether you are a member of a unitary board, a two-tier or a hybrid board, in the UK or elsewhere, the ideas in this book will be useful because conversation is at the heart of board governance across the world. So, while acknowledging the differences – described in more detail in *Conversation 2: About the board* – there are insights from various sectors, chosen because they may be useful in your context. Many of the examples are drawn from the UK – for example, from the UK Financial Reporting Council regulatory guidance – because they make a particular point which is generally relevant, even if the board you sit on is not legally required to abide by that particular piece of guidance. Because this book is intended to be useful to boards of all kinds, it uses some specific terms – for example, when the book refers to the chief executive officer or CEO, it will also be relevant to people working as the most senior executive leader in the organization, whatever their title.

But this book has been written to help you to get underneath the codes and legislation and tap into *how* boards operate. It does, of course, acknowledge the differences and similarities in the contexts of boards, whether private, public or voluntary sector, in the UK or elsewhere. There is no 'one-size-fits-all' answer because the 'law of proportionality' applies here; in some contexts, the conversations in this book will have greater significance than in others. For example, CEO remuneration in the private sector is significant both because of the financial outlay and the reputational issues arising from shareholder reactions, but in the public sector, remuneration levels are more tightly controlled and may not be under the board's control.

What the book contains

The first section offers you six *conversational techniques*, presented as a 'kitbag' of approaches you may want to use in different situations.

The rest of the book focuses on 18 *crucial conversations*, about particular topics or with particular stakeholders. Conversations are fluid, so the 18 conversations in this book aren't necessarily in the sequence that you'd expect and they have some overlaps and connections between them. However, you will find conversations to help you with the varied responsibilities of being a board member, and they can be read as 'stand-alone' guidance for specific situations.

This book contains numerous *models* to illustrate the points about the various and vital conversations that board members need to have. Some of these are well-known models, widely used, and included here because they are so useful; others are models that the authors have developed to express visually a set of ideas to help you in boardroom conversations. A visual image can be a more memorable way of encapsulating an idea, and that is important: conversations happen in the moment, and if the models are to be helpful in those moments, they must be easily recalled. Some will be of more use to you than others, depending on your particular circumstances, so you can pick and choose which to read about and which to use.

The book is designed to be accessible, but it doesn't contain all the answers you will need to be an effective board member. The conversations you should be having will give you answers, provided you can talk to the right people, at the right time and in the right way. These conversations are built around questions and attentive listening to the answers, so in some there are *checklists* of conversations-starters to help you in different situations. In others, there are checklists of possible actions, or questions to ask yourself, for your own reflection, to improve your own performance.

There are also examples – short *case studies* – of the situations that each conversation focuses on. These are drawn from real experience, some suitably anonymized to preserve confidentiality, and are intended to show you how others have faced similar issues. Some are stories in which things went wrong for lack of the right conversation at the right time.

And because board members are busy, the Introduction and each conversation contains a **summary** of the key points made in a set of easy-to-read bullet points.

Introduction:
The conversation 'kitbag'

We all know how to talk, because we do it all the time. We chat virtually, confer on conference calls, or catch up in the margins of a meeting. But the practice of *conversation* is more powerful: these are interactions that have the potential to connect people, to change minds, or to generate new ideas. They can help to repair relationships or energize a group to take action. Conversations are now so crucial in boardrooms that it's worth examining what makes them effective – or not.

Boardrooms have changed significantly in the past few decades, as *Conversation 2: About the board* describes. Their remit has widened: boards in all sectors are expected to identify and engage actively with their stakeholders and explain how they have taken account of their views in the strategy. The board must consider the impact of a wider range of issues – environmental, social and governance (ESG) matters, artificial intelligence and cyber-security, for example – all of which are rising to the top of the average board agenda. The various governance scandals affecting many sectors have increased the compliance work-load, as both regulators and the public demand that executives are held to account. The role of a board member, whether independent or executive, has become much more demanding.

Culture in the boardroom has also shifted, while conversational styles in many boardrooms lag somewhat behind. The emphasis on scrutiny and checking has to be balanced by the collaborative co-creation required of a board responsible for longer-term stew-ardship that considers the views of stakeholders.

To cope with these new demands, board members must become an agile and effective working group. This is not simple: every board is different, so even experienced board members need to adapt their approach. The board may not meet very often – perhaps four to eight board meetings a year, with limited interaction in between – so board members may not know each other well. Virtual and hybrid meetings do not make it any easier: when boards meet remotely, their interactions are more stilted, and reactions harder to judge.

All this implies that board members must 'read' the situation and the organization rapidly, and learn what kind of conversations are going to make a difference, either in formal meetings or outside. There is a growing belief that it is the behavioural interactions in the boardroom that will make a difference to the task of ensuring good governance and an effective board.

Research on boardroom interactions

Because every board is different and access is not easy, research about what happens inside boardrooms has been relatively limited. But some useful insights do emerge: for example, one study set up to contribute to the Higgs Review in 2002–2003 noted that independent board members are appointed as individuals for their specific skill sets, but then are expected to work collectively, developing strategies, scrutinizing operations and managing risk.[1]

This illustrates the complexity of the role; board members need to bring their individual and diverse skills to work effectively with colleagues whom they may not know well, in order to discharge some increasingly wide-ranging and complicated responsibilities.

The description of the ideal behaviours for independent board members further underlines the demands of the role. They need to be:

- **engaged but non-executive:** To establish themselves on the board as a credible board member, they need to engage in the business, but respect the boundaries of the executive role and cope with the information asymmetry problem;

- **challenging but supportive:** They need to bring objective challenge to the board but also to recognize their blend of 'experienced ignorance' because they will not know as much as those they are challenging. And this must be balanced with appropriate support;
- **independent but involved:** They need to operate with a level of detachment, in order to see the wood from the trees, but not be viewed as distrustful. Conveying a sense of their involvement in a collective endeavour builds trust and creates a context in which executives are more likely to be open.

These three combinations underline the point that *how* independent board members discharge their role is as important as *what* they do. And conversation is central to this.

Six conversational techniques

There are six techniques worth using in conversations round the boardroom table:

1. Framing the conversation: being an ethnographer
2. Observing: fuelling your conversations
3. Using your instincts
4. Listening
5. Questioning
6. Addressing conflict

These six might be described as the ingredients of effective boardroom conversations – techniques to have in your 'kitbag', ready to use in different situations.

Reading about these techniques will give you the opportunity to reflect on something you do regularly as a board member at every board meeting: talking with fellow board members and with staff, both inside and outside the boardroom. Reflecting on your practice is one of the keys to improvement, and each section offers some questions to help you to do this.

Technique 1 – Framing the conversation: Being an ethnographer

> 'Culture hides much more than it reveals, and strangely enough, what it hides, it hides most effectively from its own participants'.
>
> Edward T. Hall, *The silent language* (1959, p.39)

To be effective, board members must understand the context of the organization, particularly its culture. The board will have its own particular culture, too, and board members must work within it to get things done. But the actions they take, and the conversations they have, also affect and shape the culture of the whole organization, for better or worse.

Gauging the culture of an organization is best done through observation – and this is an ethnographic skill, necessary for both scrutiny and strategizing. Ethnographers live in the societies they are observing and describing, in the same way as board members 'live' in the organization their board is part of.

The culture web is a framework to help board members to examine the culture of an organization, and to understand the significance of what they observe. It is useful in various ways: for new board members in learning about the organization they will oversee, or in merger and acquisition decisions where the cultural fit between two organizations is a key success factor. It is often used in transformation projects which involve a degree of culture change, too.

Figure I.1 illustrates six areas for observation in your interactions with the board, or when you are visiting the organization.

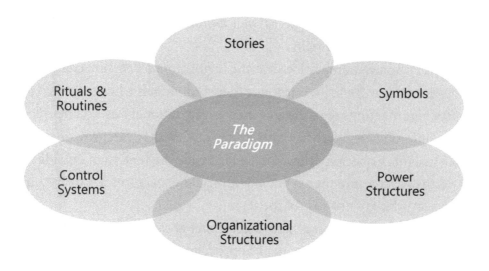

Figure I.1   Six areas of observation[2]

Listen for the *stories* that people tell you, about what has happened in the past and why, about their successes and their failures. These tell you about what is valued in this organization. Often, these are stories about individuals who fought against the cultural norms – for example, the outstanding sales person who railed against being part of a team but was rewarded anyway.

Look at some *symbols* – the artefacts and physical objects in the workplace. These tell you what people care about – or what they are supposed to care about. What's on the noticeboards? In one financial services company, the noticeboards contained out-of-date calendars and lists of rules and procedures, whereas in the staff room of a school, they were full of photographs of a recent charity event, and both were clues to the culture. The same goes for the virtual objects, such as the organization's staff intranet or communications newsletter – what do they tell you about what matters in this organization?

Even in the early weeks, your conversations will tell you about the *power structures* inside the organization. Is this a hierarchical organiza-tion where managers have offices and members of staff dress formally, for example? In one international bank, members of staff were always introduced with their grade as well as their name, underlining the importance of the hierarchy.

Every board member looks at the *organization structure* chart, but how does this work in practice? Are there individuals who are invited to particular meetings regardless of their organizational position because their opinion is regularly sought? It may be that they can provide valuable insights or because they are 'better inside the tent' than outside it. And the reverse: are there people you would expect to see involved in a project who are not part of the team?

You will also see and hear indications about the *control systems* in place, the set of management approaches used to get things done and to regulate activity. Are people given targets which they have to achieve, for example, with regular reporting on progress? Who gets bonuses and what for? Talk to members of staff about how performance is managed; the performance appraisal process is a particular feature of control structures that can have enormous implications for organizational culture. Do members of staff have regular performance discussions, and are they linked to development?

And then there are the processes you observe, the *rituals and routines* which occur regularly. For example, are there team meetings each week, or only when there is a particular crisis or announcement? Look for the contradictions, too: for example, an organization focused on improving efficiency which also allows senior people to take time off for their own ventures during the summer.

Seeing clearly

There is increasing awareness of the importance of these so-called soft cultural issues which make such a difference in organizations. For example, Gillian Tett, in her book *Anthro-vision*, writes about the silo structures and consequent tunnel vision inside banks that contributed to the financial crash of 2018.[3] She observed that bankers seemed not to see the users at the end of the chain of transactions, nor did they have an aggregated view of their risks. She suggests some other ways

to understand more clearly what is happening inside an organi
including:

- **listening for the social silences:** The topics that seem never to get discussed, but which may be more important than what is talked about;
- **joining the dots:** Looking for the links between decisions and their impact on people in their cultural and social context;
- **looking for the gap:** Noticing the difference between what is said and what is done;
- **taking a non-judgemental approach:** Moving slowly to judgement once you understand more about what is really happening and why.

Reflections on Technique 1

- What are the symbols and rituals of your organization?
- What stories are told in the organization and what does that tell you about what is valued?
- How would you describe the culture in the boardroom? Does it model the values of the organization?
- How diverse is your board?
- Are there any social silences in your boardroom?

Technique 2 – Observing: Fuelling your conversations

The clearer your observations of the organization, the board and your context, the better your understanding will be. That will inform boardroom conversations and make the board's oversight more effective. James Gilmore, in his book *Look: A practical guide for improving your observational skills*, describes six different lenses to use in observing what goes on inside and outside the boardroom. Table I.1 sets out how this idea can be adapted for use in boardroom conversations, and also offers some example observations in specific situations.[4]

Table I.1   Six lenses for board members

Lens	Purpose	Example Observations
Binoculars	To look across and survey at a distance. Particularly useful for strategy and forward planning (see *Conversation 6: About strategy* and *Conversation 7: About the future*).	Where does the organization sit in the market place? How is it viewed by the regulator?
Bifocals	To look between two contrasting views or directions alternately. Useful for conversations with stakeholders (see *Conversation 13: With stakeholders*).	How does the finance director approach things and how does it compare with the sales director? What keeps each of them awake at night?
Magnifying glasses	To look closely at one main spot. Particularly useful in holding to account (see *Conversation 8: About holding to account*).	How does the organization recognize income – where is judgement being made? What do the auditors say?
Microscopes	To look around for more and greater details. Useful for holding to account and in a crisis to study and scrutinize the situation (see *Conversation 18: About a crisis*).	The absenteeism figures are rising – sickness due to mental health in particular. What's really going on here?

Rose-coloured glasses	To look at the possibly hidden potential of something, seeing it as it could be. Useful in strategy development (see *Conversation 6: About strategy*).	Our new product line is still under development but could we sell direct to customers as well as businesses?
Blindfolds	To look back and recall. Useful for board member reflection on meetings, decisions and the effectiveness of the board overall (see *Conversation 10: About effectiveness*).	What did I observe during my visit today?

Adapted from Gilmore (2016, p.14).

The advice is to select the right kind of lens for the task in hand – whether it is a strategy discussion, or part of the regular scrutiny role of a board. This range of approaches is a useful reminder of the importance of consciously taking different perspectives in board discussions and engaging in different kinds of conversations.

Reflections on Technique 2

- What is there about the organization that you don't really understand? What will you put under the *microscope*?
- When you reflect on board meetings: put on the *blindfold*. Did you see a willingness to be challenged and space for different views to be heard? What is the level of energy? Does it feel like a meeting that is adding value where there is openness to challenge? How would you describe relationships? What does the body language look like?

- With your *bifocals* on, how does this organization compare with other organizations you are familiar with?

Technique 3 – Using your instincts

Board members spend time examining data in board packs, supplementing this with their observations of the organization and the people in it. They also use their instincts, feelings or reactions based on their experiences. This combination is part of the skill of being a board member – but there must be a balance. Gut feel, or instinct, may seem inappropriate in a boardroom conversation but the reaction is worth surfacing to see what it tells you. Your reflections may encourage you to talk to your board colleagues if something *'just doesn't feel right'* – and there is more about this in *Conversation 4: With board members*.

In her book *Fierce conversations*, Susan Scott sets out a way of surfacing and using your instincts to probe appropriately.[5] She points out the importance of articulating clearly what your instinct is telling you, and then formulating a way of expressing this in conversation. Her approach is illustrated in Table I.2: the left-hand column logs your private thoughts, while the right-hand column allows you to express that thought constructively, in a way which won't generate defensiveness.[6]

To take an example: an instinctive reaction such as *'They say they will deliver this on time, but I am not so sure'* may be hard to articulate, for a range of reasons: not wanting to appear negative or to hold up the meeting, or not wanting to look stupid in front of colleagues with more experience. But, by bringing your instinct into the neutral zone, in the middle column of Table I.2, you can notice your instinctive reaction without attachment to it. This will help you to formulate the question or comment publicly as an observation. This 'perception checking' lets people know what is on your mind, but does not generate defensiveness because your comment is not positioned as any sort of truth.

Table I.2   From instinctive reaction to expression

Private thought	Neutral thought	Public thought
'I don't feel they are really committed to this deadline'.

'They have said not to worry about subsidiary N from a regulatory point of view but they also said that about the international business which is giving us all sorts of worries'. | You are aware of what you think and feel it without attachment.

You don't claim your private thought is right or wrong – you want to share it to see if it brings any insight into the conversation. | 'I may be wrong but I feel there is some hesitancy about meeting this deadline'.

'We are focusing our effort on international business, and I just want to reconfirm the assumption that subsidiary N is okay'. |

Being able to voice your instinctive concerns may take courage, particularly in a time-constrained board meeting. But failing to surface them may leave the board vulnerable to what is called the 'corporate nod'. This occurs when board members do not express their anxieties, even when asked, because of fear, lack of experience or a desire not to waste time. Then, when the chair asks each board member if they agree, one by one the board members nod – even though all their concerns may not have been addressed.

Reflections on Technique 3

- Have you seen the 'corporate nod' in your board meeting?
- Is there a situation when you were able to use your instinctive reaction to ask a question or make an observation?
- Have you seen a colleague on the board do this well? Less well?

Technique 4 – Listening

It is a cliché to say that we each have two ears and one mouth and that they should be used in those proportions, but it is also powerfully true. And, on that basis, independent board members should probably have four eyes, four ears and one mouth.

Being an independent board member presents all sorts of listening opportunities: at the boardroom table, or in meetings with executives, in conversations with members of staff or with stakeholders. But there is real pressure to talk, too – in order to demonstrate your value to the board, or perhaps to help to solve the problem at hand by talking about your previous experience.

Although this is understandable and a common experience, talking without listening can be damaging. Good listening is part of the ethnographic observations you make, and allows your instincts to be turned up.

From time to time, it's worth assessing your own listening skills, as Scott sets out, so take some time to reflect on how often you find yourself:

- formulating what you want to say while someone else is talking;
- responding immediately with little or no thought;
- focusing on whether your contribution will impress others;
- interrupting with a solution before the problem has been completely described;
- using silence or a break in the conversation to change the subject;
- talking in circles, going over the same ground;
- monopolizing the conversation with a monologue;
- talking while you work out what it is you want to say.[7]

Occasionally, we may all find ourselves doing some of these, often for the best of reasons, but they are ineffective contributions to the conversations and get in the way of listening.

Listening to someone is a way of increasing your ability to influence and yet strangely we often forget that.[8]

One of the themes running through this book is to encourage independent board members to use some of the skills employed by executive coaches. Don't be fooled into thinking that coaching is soft, self-indulgent and inappropriate for a boardroom; these are powerful conversations that will support the board in delivering a vision, driving performance and holding to account. But all good coaching starts with good listening and that skill is the absolute foundation of being an effective board member. By being a good listener, you can go beyond what is said and listen for what is not said – or *'perhaps you hear a change in the person's tone of voice or something in their words that doesn't quite ring true... pick up on subtleties that can easily be missed by casual attention or listening'.*[9]

In her book on coaching, Julie Starr identifies several levels of listening, which are illustrated in Figure I.2.

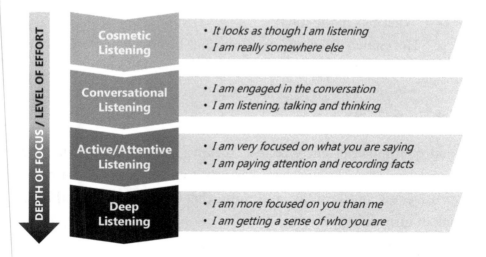

Figure I.2   Levels of listening

Adapted from Starr (2016, p.61).

Conversational listening is what most of us do most of the time – for most of us, it is a natural activity – but as a board member, attentive and deep listening will deliver much more insight. When someone listens attentively, they regularly confirm that they are listening, ask clarifying questions, repeat and summarize information. Sometimes, people even write down what they hear, which gives the speaker solid evidence that they are being listened to.

With deep listening, there is a sense of intention – '*I really want to understand this*'. The listener's mind is quiet, but they also tune into their instincts with no attempt to analyze what things mean at this stage.

This kind of listening generates positive reactions – it makes people feel heard and encourages them to talk freely. And that, in turn, creates the kinds of conversations which board members need to be effective.

Reflections on Technique 4

- How would you rate your listening skills?
- What gets in the way?
- How much listening goes on in your boardroom? Do you have board colleagues who are particularly good listeners?

Technique 5 – Questioning

Good questions can energize the executive, stimulate creativity and unearth concerns. By contrast, a poorly framed question can cause defensiveness and hostility, and mean that information is withheld. That, in turn, destroys trust.

Questioning and listening are at the heart of coaching techniques and they are the foundations of effective boardroom conversations. Powerful questions are open-ended, and aim to empower the person answering rather than closing a topic down. They create possibilities and encourage discovery. They are non-judgemental and are designed to create a shared understanding.

But careful formulation of the question is key here. One example, drawn from sports coaching, illustrates the importance of exactly how the question is formulated. When something went wrong in a tennis match, the coach did not ask '*what went wrong with that shot?*' but instead asked a question intended to invite observation (back to Technique 2): '*how high was the ball above the net?*' This question is non-judgemental, asks for a descriptive answer, prompts the player to reflect on what they saw, and, in future matches, makes them watch the ball more closely. It allows a feedback loop – because the observation can be verified, given that the coach can also see how high the ball was. All this clarifies the current issue and fuels improved performance next time.[10]

In a board context, this idea translates into questions like: *What does success look like – how will we know if this has been done correctly? What is the biggest obstacle you've experienced so far and what did you do to overcome it?*

Formulating the right questions is the first step, but sometimes the second question is the key to unlocking the situation, so board members shouldn't feel that they are only allowed one question per issue. A follow-up question is always worth the time taken, to ensure that the issue is understood.

And the key to all of this is creating the atmosphere in which it is acceptable to answer with '*I don't know*'. It is very dangerous to operate in an environment where executives feel that they have to make up the answers and then stick to them, even if they learn immediately after the meeting that the answer was wrong. In one project approval meeting, the senior executive was asked about the date for users to be able to test the live system and confidently said '*April*'. His team were appalled – April was the date for the start of basic system testing within the project team, not for involving users. But the senior executive, needing to save face, instructed them to accelerate the work, thus increasing the cost and risk. It would have been so much better to be able to check the schedule in front of them, ask a member of the team to reply, or even to say '*let me get the latest information and get back to you*'.

Reflections on Technique 5

- Does your board regularly ask questions that generate discussion, rather than short answers?
- Are your questions framed broadly enough, to generate a full answer? Do you ask the second, follow-up question sometimes, to be sure that the board understands?
- Do executives see the questions as constructive? How do you know?

Technique 6 – Addressing conflict

Both experience and research indicate that conflict in conversations is often not addressed, or even avoided. People sometimes succumb to the social and psychological pressure to remain silent in conversation with others who they believe are more knowledgeable or who have more experience. They feel that expressing a contrary view might weaken the group's connections or be seen as bad manners. But this brings real risks to boards, as set out in *Conversation 17: About risk*.

But boards need different views and disagreement is sometimes necessary. Boards need to hear the varied views of people with diverse backgrounds and experiences, because complex situations can often only be fully understood from a range of different perspectives. The problem arises when disagreement becomes prolonged and turns into conflict.

Individual board members need to balance the expression of their own views with the board's need to act collectively as one effective working group. The framework in Figure I.3 illustrates how the balance between assertive expression of views and the need for co-operative behaviour may play out.

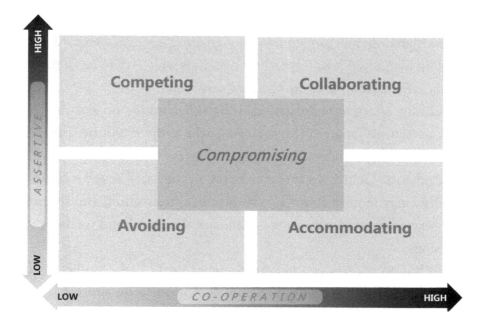

Figure I.3 Balancing assertion and co-operation

Adapted from Davey (2019, p.39).

Davey's framework underlines the point that conflict avoidance is the biggest risk, particularly where it becomes a default mode of operating. This is the realm of the 'corporate nod', described above, where board meetings start to feel like empty rituals, simply rubber-stamping decisions, because no one wants to express an alternative view and there is little sense of the necessity for co-operative interaction in the group.

But there are other risks, too. Where there are board members with a strong desire to express their own views, there can be a sense that independent board members are in some way *competing* with executives, thus generating conflict. The response to this is well-intentioned, timely feedback, and there is more on this below. It may be that the differences in view require *compromising* on some matters, and that may not necessarily be a bad thing if it allows some progress. If board members have a high need for co-operation, though, their discussions may simply result in bland, vague or impractical decisions which try to be all things to all people, *accommodating* contradictory views.

Ideally, effective boards need to be *collaborating* on key matters such as setting longer-term strategies, where there will be different views from stakeholders, including employees and suppliers as well as regulators. Getting to this collaboration may well involve conflict and this may require courage to resolve in conversation. The alternative – avoidance or abdication – damages the board and weakens its decisions.

Failing to address conflict creates what Davey calls 'conflict debt': the sum of all the contentious issues that need to be addressed but which are never discussed and remain unresolved. Conflict debt can be exacerbated even by simply withholding the feedback that would allow a colleague to do a better job, or by continually deferring a strategic decision while falling further and further behind the competition.

So, why don't we address these matters when they arise? There are numerous reasons, and there is more about this in *Conversation 17: About risk*. Some are about individual issues: anxieties about weakening an important relationship, concern about hurting feelings, or fearing some form of retaliation. Some are a function of the culture in the boardroom: bitter experience may have taught board members that a confrontation could escalate the problem rather than resolve it, or generate an outcome that might be worse than the issue itself.[11]

The conversational key to addressing conflict is *feedback* – constructively talking about what's just happened. This may be mainly a job for the chair, and there is more on this in *Conversation 10: About effectiveness*, but individual board members are also part of conversations that can address this. There are two particular elements in these conversations that contribute to their effectiveness:

1. First, providing a context for the feedback: literally describing when, where and what was observed. For example, '*Yesterday in the board meeting, I heard you say... and you were clearly upset about this...*'. This allows the other person to visualize the time and place you are referring to.

2. Then, exploring the issue: '*Can you tell me more about what was happening and why?*'

This approach opens up the issue and may create the space for further feedback about other reactions to it. Or, it may not: the person may simply deny that anything happened, defend their position or deflect the conversation onto another subject. But in addressing such situations, board members also need to ask themselves some key questions:

- Would my intervening help this situation or make it worse?
- Do I have a perspective on the issue that will help open up potential solutions?
- Could I use my credibility or influence to make the situation better?

Reflections on Technique 6

How are potentially contentious issues brought to your board?

- Is it through a tightly controlled, time-limited discussion?
- Or is it a full debate? Are views from everyone invited?
- Are there one or two people who disagree all the time?
- Do you reach a conclusion on action or do debates endlessly swirl around?
- Is there a dependence on one or two people to make the decisions?

Case study: The need to contribute

The board of an educational organization had managed to recruit an independent board member from an IT background. But he rarely spoke in meetings, unless the topic was directly relevant to his experience. When he did contribute, he tended to push forward IT solutions that had been adopted in his last company, where he had held a senior executive role *(competing)*.

At one meeting, the board had a particularly difficult decision to make about an acquisition with financial, regulatory and IT implications. He made no contribution. After the meeting, he sent an email to the chair, to explain why he thought the board had made the wrong decision. He said that he had not wished to bring this up during the meeting *(avoiding)*, but felt it was important to let the chair know his view. He emphasized that if the chair chose to ignore his advice, he could not be held responsible.

The chair had to give some careful feedback because the board needed his IT expertise and this board member had clearly misunderstood the role if he thought he could abdicate all responsibility.

Summary

- Although we all know how to talk, conversation that connects and convinces is more important than ever in boards.
- There is a growing belief that it is the behavioural interactions in the boardroom that will make a difference to the task of ensuring good governance and an effective board.
- There are six particular techniques – key ingredients in effective boardroom conversations – worth having in your 'kitbag'.

- Technique 1: Framing the conversation – being an ethnographer who observes the culture of the organization from within it.
- Technique 2: Observing through six lenses fuels these conversations, looking through: *binoculars* to survey the landscape; *bifocals* to understand different perspectives; *magnifying glasses* to focus attention on key issues; *microscopes* to look for more and greater detail; *rose-coloured glasses* to see hidden potential in something; and *blindfolds*, as part of reflection.
- Technique 3: Using your instincts: surfacing and using your instincts to probe appropriately.
- Technique 4: Listening – cosmetic, conversational, active and attentive or deep listening.
- Technique 5: Questioning – asking powerful questions that allow honest answers, and following up with the second question that gets to the heart of the issue.
- Technique 6: Addressing conflict through conversations that offer feedback, so that the board's *conflict debt* doesn't become unmanageable.

Checklist: Techniques to use in conversation

For each of the 18 crucial conversations explored in this book, board members should consider:

Technique	
1	Putting on an ethnographer's hat.
2	Selecting the most appropriate observational lens.
3	Using your instincts.
4	Listening deeply.
5	Asking powerful questions.
6	Addressing conflict.

About joining: Understanding the role of a board member

As you decide whether or not to take on a board position, there are some key questions that you need to answer yourself, or to find answers from others, through your conversations.

Board roles are an opportunity to make a difference, but they are also more onerous and demanding than they used to be, as *Conversation 2: About the board* sets out. Workloads have increased and the balance of risk and reward has altered. As a result, some people decide to find other ways to use their expertise or to give back to society.

Joining a board is not a decision to take lightly. It is worth doing your own 'due diligence' on the organization and its board, but also on your own motivations and circumstances.

Four due diligence conversations

There are four kinds of conversation that are worth having about the decision to join a board – or not.

Reflecting on your own reasons for applying and what you are looking for in a board role is fundamental – hence the need for a conversation with *yourself* at the outset. This will help you to decide whether to apply for a board role; it will also help you if you do apply, because you will be asked questions about your motivation and what you have to offer during the recruitment process.

Most importantly, you will want to find the opportunity to talk to *board members* of the particular organization you are considering. This might be built into the recruitment process, but an early conversation will help you to answer some of the key questions set out below.

It is also useful to talk to *board members on other boards*, in different organizations or sectors, to compare the different contexts. Some may suit your expertise better than others, because board members contribute in different ways and focus on different aspects of the role.

Finally, you will want to know whether this organization is regarded as successful and how it is viewed externally. So, if you can find the opportunity to talk to a *stakeholder* – a major supplier, or even a competitor – it will give you some insight.

Ten questions to answer

These four conversations will help you to answer 10 key questions as part of the process of joining a board.

Q1: Why join a board?

You are the person best placed to answer the question '*why do you want to be a member of a board?*' What's the contribution you want to make and are you the right person to make it?

Talking to board members in other sectors or on other types of board will help you to clarify your own aspirations. What do they have to tell you about their experience of being a board member – whether that is as a trustee, member of an advisory board or a company non-executive? What do they like? What is difficult? Do they find it fulfilling?

Q2: What kind of board do you want to join?

Board structures vary by sector and board members spend their time in different ways depending on the organization.

- Company boards are heavily regulated and directors carry legal accountability for the actions of the organization. The board will usually be a combination of executive and non-executive directors, with a range of skills and specific roles in the committee structure (see *Conversation 2: About the board*).

- Professional services firms range from public corporations to traditional partnerships. In some firms, the board will consist of partners with ownership responsibility, with independent members who are unlikely to have legal or fiduciary duties. Here the role of an independent board member will tend to be as expert business adviser, consultant or facilitator.

- Charity boards often consist entirely of independent board members, with the CEO only 'in attendance' at its meetings, rather than as a member of it. They may often face complex stakeholder issues, or undertake functions formerly undertaken by the state and so receive government funding. Although the charity's purpose will be the cornerstone of the board's work, the search for funding may drive diversification, and donor activity requires scrutiny.

- Public bodies such as government departments, executive agencies, or other arm's-length bodies often have independent members on the board. They tend to be recruited for their private-sector experience, and may well have little or no formal legal or fiduciary duty. Such boards may be chaired by the relevant secretary of state, by a civil servant or an appointed lead non-executive. These boards may not have the full range of governance functions – for example, strategy may be driven by ministerial views as part of the political process – but they offer the opportunity to contribute to important work.

- Universities will generally have representatives from the staff and students on their boards; these are board director appointments and whilst they are there to ensure the voices of these stakeholders are taken into account, they are not there to 'represent' their respective constituencies. The challenge here is to ensure that the board is able to engage with the academic mission of the institution.
- School governing bodies in the state sector have a range of collective responsibilities and should expect to be assessed for their leadership and management as part of the school inspection regime. In the independent sector, these boards are either charity boards or company boards.

You may already know people who serve on different boards, but if you are looking for someone to talk with, the associations, trade bodies or various institutes may be able to advise, and the *Appendix* offers some sources of information to help you.

Q3: What is the role?

Board membership, particularly as an independent member, non-executive or trustee, can be the opportunity to put your previous experience to good use in a different organization.

However, it is also a different kind of role from that of an executive leader and you will need to approach it differently. Most boards meet only at scheduled intervals and their role is not about day-to-day management as part of a team, but about governance, working in collaboration with board colleagues. Some people find this less fulfilling than they expected; others relish the opportunity to step into a completely different role.

This may or may not be what you are looking for at this stage of your life. If you have had a long career as an executive, you will certainly have experience to offer, but ask yourself whether you want to take on this different kind of role. This is the 'governance or golf?' question: how do you want to spend your time?

Q4: What is the role like in practice?

Conversations with other members of this board will tell you about the reality of doing the job. It is useful to understand what kind of role existing board members play – are they genuinely independent board members bringing an outside perspective, or are they appointed by particular stakeholder groups? What is the balance of executive and non-executive or independent members on the board? Do you get the sense that the independent board members can make a real contribution or are they merely decorative, fig-leaf appointments intended to make the board appear properly structured and externally connected?

Most board members will tell you that the time requirement set out in the job description almost always understates the actual time required to do the job properly. You will want to be sure that you have sufficient time to discharge the role well.

Serving as an independent board member may well require you to change the way you work. Stepping up to the board from an executive role is a significant transition, and even more so if you move to a board in a different sector than your current role. For example, if you are an experienced executive in the private sector, you will need to operate differently if you become a board member of a public-sector body. The role is different, and its processes and culture will be too, because it is an organization designed to serve citizens and the government of the day.

Q5: What's the balance of risk and reward in this role?

There is a personal reputational risk attached to board membership in any sector, which will be largely out of your control. Taking on such a role might enhance your reputation but, if something goes wrong, the board will be held accountable – as will you: a problem arising in the organization you serve may make it harder for you to be appointed to other roles, even if the problem was not directly under your control or of your making. As a board member, you will spend less time inside the organization than executives, and have less information to work with, but, unless this is a purely advisory role, you will be accountable for what happens.

On the other hand, a board role can be an opportunity to be involved in something you care about and to make a real difference, working with able and committed people. Board roles bring other rewards, too: financial, the chance to raise your profile, or as a stepping stone to other jobs. Ask yourself what you are looking for, and examine the risk:reward ratio.

Q6: Is this organization worth joining?

To answer this question, talk to someone with experience of the organization – a key customer or service user, or someone from a trade body or association. For example, if you are thinking of becoming a school governor, talk to more than one parent to get their perspectives. Alternatively, talk to someone in your network who serves on the board of a comparable organization, obviously acknowledging and avoiding the competitive issue. The insight you gain from each of these conversations will, of course, be from one particular viewpoint, so you will want to triangulate it with other opinions. This includes doing your own research on the organization in social media: look at Glassdoor for example to see what employees say about working in the organization (www.glassdoor.com).

Q7: What do you have to offer this organization?

You will certainly be asked this question at interview and your answer will be better for the research you have done in these preparatory conversations. For example, you may have an interest in the work of the organization or experience of using its services, but the key question to ask yourself is whether you can make a valuable contribution – and what this organization needs from board members. This requires research: for example, about changes in their market place, regulatory issues they may be facing, or about their future plans or new developments – because these may be areas where your experience could be useful.

Q8: Will you be able to work with your board colleagues?

Often, as part of the interview process, there will be an opportunity to talk to other members of the board you are applying for. They will see this as part of their interview process, but it is also part of your due diligence. They will be assessing you in your conversation, but you want to be sure you can work effectively with them and with this organization.

You will want to be sure that you can see yourself collaborating effectively with them in the service of the organization. Do these look like people you can trust? Levels of trust between board members may fluctuate from time to time at critical moments, but if you have any doubt about this at the outset, proceed only with caution.

Q9: How will the recruitment and induction process work?

The recruitment process is very revealing: the way your application is handled and the way you are interviewed will tell you a great deal about what this organization will be like to work for. Public-sector recruitment, for example, is different from private-sector processes: the time-table will be longer, the process more formal, and application form and interviews will be structured tightly around the job description.

Ask about the arrangements for induction and what other training may be offered to you, if you are appointed. For example, some boards operate a 'buddy system', pairing a new board member with a longer-standing member, to give them the chance to get a fellow board member's perspective and to speed up the induction process. If the induction you are offered doesn't look useful enough, set up some other meetings – as described in *Conversation 5: About the organization* – so that you don't miss the window of opportunity to learn about this organization at the start of your term of office.

Q10: What are the specific terms and conditions?

Although many job advertisements set out the terms and conditions, you will need to be clear about some of the details. For example, some public-sector boards require board members to record their time and submit it monthly as a basis for the payment of the fee. Most private-sector boards pay their non-executives through the payroll system every month, while many charity trustees receive no remuneration at all, but are sometimes allowed to claim for their travelling expenses.

Some boards set up performance contracts for independent board members, outlining the expectations of the role in terms of contribution, attendance and ethics. Although they may only be employed as a final option in the event of a dispute, they will probably form part of regular effectiveness reviews, as discussed in *Conversation 10: About effectiveness*.

And one important question, which is often omitted, is to ask about Directors' and Officers' professional indemnity insurance arrangements. You may never need to know this but it's still worth asking.

Case study: Researching a new organization

One experienced non-executive was considering applying for a board position in a new public body, due to be established later that year. With no other board members appointed and only a few members of senior staff in place, there was limited opportunity to research the organization and the role. Instead, he talked to people who had been involved in setting up new public bodies, albeit in completely different sectors, to ask about their roles. He also looked at organizations with a similar remit abroad. Although none of these conversations was directly relevant, they helped him to decide whether he might have something to contribute to this new organization, and to prepare for the interview.

Summary

- Board membership is both a demanding and rewarding role. There are four conversations which might help you to decide whether to apply for board membership and what sort of board you want to join:
  - first, a reflective conversation with yourself; and then conversations with
  - board members from other organizations in any sector;
  - board members from the particular organization you are thinking of joining;
  - some of its external stakeholders.
- These conversations are part of your own due diligence and they will help you to answer 10 important questions:
  - Q1: Why join a board?
  - Q2: What kind of board do you want to join?
  - Q3: What is the role?
  - Q4: What is the role like in practice?
  - Q5: What is the balance of risk and reward in this role?
  - Q6: Is this organization worth joining?
  - Q7: What do you have to offer this organization?
  - Q8: Will you be able to work with your board colleagues?
  - Q9: How will the recruitment and induction process work?
  - Q10: What are the specific terms and conditions?

- You will get a range of different views from your preparatory conversations, and you will obviously need to triangulate them as you come to your own conclusions about joining a board.
- Recruitment processes can tell you much about what this organization and this board will be like. In your interview, they will be assessing you, but you will want to be sure that you can trust this group of people and work with them effectively.

Checklist: Conversational topics

Here is a list of conversational prompts and questions to help you get the most from these useful conversations.

Conversation with:	Question	Topics to explore
Yourself	Why do I want to be a member of a board?	What am I looking for in investing time and energy in this role? Are there other types of roles to consider (e.g., consulting roles)?
	What's the contribution I want to make?	Is my previous experience relevant and useful to this organization – and, if so, why?
	Do I have sufficient time?	Most board roles take more time than is set out in the job description. Do I have time for the published commitment of time plus, say, 30% more?
	What kind of board should I join?	Private, public or voluntary sector? A company or a charity? An advisory board, or with legal responsibilities?

Conversation with:	Question	Topics to explore
	What kind of reward am I seeking?	Financial, fulfilment, profile raising, contributing, or as a stepping stone?
	What are the risks in this role?	Personal, reputational, financial?
	Am I ready to take on a governance role, rather than a management role?	Do I understand the limits of this role – the 'eyes on, hands off' character of board oversight? Will that be fulfilling?
	Why do I want to join this particular board and what do they want in terms of time and contribution?	Have I read the person specification to understand what they need from this board member specifically? If this isn't a new role, why did the previous incumbent leave?
Board members of the particular organization	Why did they choose to join this board?	Explore their reasons for taking a position on this board. What have they done since joining?
	What works well on the board and what works less well?	Reflections on the way this particular board operates will give you an idea of whether you want to contribute in this environment and whether you can do so

Conversation with:	Question	Topics to explore
	What are the relationships round the boardroom table like?	Particularly about working relationships between the executive and the independent members, as well as with the chair
	How much challenge is there in the board's discussions and how much support? Do they feel that's an appropriate balance?	Are discussions acrimonious or cosy?
	What's the history of the organization?	Can board members tell the story of the organization, where it has come from and what is planned for the future? Have there been crises in its history and how were they dealt with?
	What arrangements are there for induction and training for new board members?	Explore how much time they may take, and how much contact you will have with employees as well as senior leaders
Members of other boards	Why did they choose to become a board member, and how did they find the right board to join?	Ask them about their motivation and the route they took to board membership
	Has the role been as they expected – in terms of time, involvement, reward and risk?	What did they expect? How much explanation were they given at the outset?

Conversation with:	Question	Topics to explore
	What do they like about the board they work with? Is there anything they find frustrating?	
External stakeholders	What is it like to work with this organization or to use its services?	For example, is the organization easy to deal with, and does it provide an efficient service?
	What do other organizations say about this organization? What is its reputation?	How is this organization regarded in the sector – for example, as a major player or market leader, or with a reputation for innovation?

About the board: Exploring the role of this board

As you join the board, you will want to understand more about the scope of its work and how you will spend your time. This conversation will help you to see how and why your board operates as it does – and you may need to look at both theory and practice: the ideas that underpin the structure of boards, and how they shape the way the board operates.

There are three key ideas here:

1. the changes in the remit of boards over time;
2. how that alters the conversations around a boardroom table;
3. the importance of understanding the implications for your particular board.

The changing remit of the board

'Society is demanding that companies, both public and private, serve a social purpose. To prosper over time, every company must not only deliver financial performance, but also show how it makes a positive contribution to society. Companies must benefit all their stakeholders, including shareholders, employees, customers and the communities in which they operate'.

(Larry Fink, Blackrock, 2018 letter to CEOs,

www.nytimes.com)

This quotation illustrates the changing view of what a company is and what it does – and boards in other sectors also see their remit altering in the same way. This shift is still under way, although at different speeds, driven by economic and environmental pressure, corporate scandals and changes in society. Board members need to understand how to operate within this broader remit, as it applies in their particular context.

The aim of a board

Ideas about what boards do, and why, have developed over time, and some history and a little theory will help you to understand how and why boards work as they do.

To put it simply: board structures appear to have come into play when the owner or owners of an organization no longer wished to run it directly themselves; there may have been too many owners to work effectively together; or the organization's work has grown to be so complex that some form of closer, central management is needed. Thus, the board becomes the agent of the owner(s), and independent board members are appointed to ensure that the agents complied with instructions and maximized returns. This is the essence of *agency theory*, which is the foundation for much of the corporate governance in the UK and US. This idea is built on the separation between the ownership of a business and the individuals employed to manage it.[12]

The underlying assumptions of this approach to governance can play out in the way board members talk to each other and to executives. The theory assumes that:

- people always act in their own best interests;

- and the interests of owners (shareholders) and managers are likely to differ;
- so, governance mechanisms are necessary to bring these interests into alignment;
- and, therefore, independent board directors are an essential monitoring device to ensure that the problems of this separation are minimized.

These assumptions put the emphasis on conforming and the monitoring role of the board and drive conversations that are primarily about scrutiny of what is being done.[13]

Now, however, organizations focus much more on broader value creation, and so *stakeholder theory* has begun to dominate in governance thinking. This view makes the board's role broader and more complex: board members must understand and consider the views of all those with a stake in the organization. In some sectors, they must also manage the trade-offs between the interests of shareholders and those of other stakeholders. Conversations round the boardroom table change: they are broader discussions, bringing in a range of external views, and the decision-making process is often more difficult because of the need to balance different requirements. Sometimes, stakeholder organizations may even have a representative on the board, although this is more complicated in practice than it seems; the board member role involves acting in the interests of the organization rather than of one constituency, no matter who has nominated them to the board.[14]

The third theoretical perspective, *stewardship theory*, was developed to challenge the notion that managers are self-interested and always acting in their own best interest. Instead, this theory assumes that board members and managers will direct their efforts to align with the organization they are part of, thereby working together to develop strategy and to monitor performance.[15]

The implicit assumption here is that the owners of the business are prepared to trust those who manage it and this changes the conversation again. The discussions round the boardroom table will be less about scrutiny of current operations and more about exploring and understanding the organization's wider impact on its community.

Board governance in practice

There are essentially two types of board governance across the world in different sectors. First, most common in the UK and US, there is a *unitary board*, consisting of both executive and non-executive directors, working together as a unified group. Second, there is a *two-tier board*, where a supervisory board oversees the work of a management board; its main task will be to appoint and dismiss members of the management board and to monitor their performance.[16] Sometimes, the board may be a hybrid of these two, as for example in some European boards or in charity boards composed solely of non-executive independent trustees. Many of the examples in this book draw on the experience of unitary, or *one-tier*, boards, but the insights in this book will apply whatever the structure.

The new challenge

Although there are numerous other theoretical definitions of boards and why they exist, these three particularly affect what board members do and how they do it today.

Agency theory has dominated for decades, even in organizations without a shareholder seeking a return. The board's work is focused on the need to check for compliance, and on delivering operational results, whether that means profit, income or services delivered. But now, the growing influence of stakeholder theory drives boards to consider the needs of other stakeholders beside the shareholder, and, as part of this, to develop higher trust partnerships inside and outside the board. And there is an expectation that organizations will focus on the delivery of longer-term results, which benefit shareholders, stakeholders and society at large.

This is the challenge for 21st-century boards: they are still required to exercise their supervisory role with an agency mindset, but also to exercise stewardship, while taking account of the needs of a wider range of stakeholders – in other words, to take all three approaches simultaneously, as Figure 2.1 illustrates.

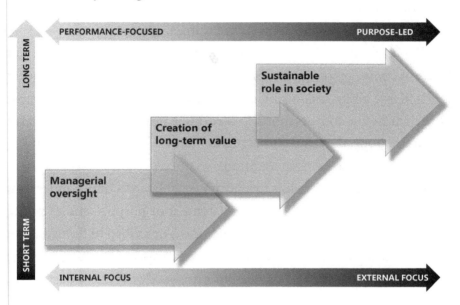

Figure 2.1   The broadening remit for boards

You can see this broadening remit in the codes and regulatory guidance which apply in different sectors: for example, the principles in the UK Corporate Governance Code (2018) require that the board '... *promote the long-term sustainable success of the company, generating value for shareholders and contributing to wider society*' and also '... *ensure that the necessary resources are in place for the company to meet its objectives and measure performance against them*'. In the same way, the Charity Governance Code (2020) emphasizes that the board must engage with stakeholders with sufficient information so that they can '*measure the charity's success in achieving its purposes*'.[17]

Theory into practice

As a result of this challenge, in many boardrooms, you will see all three approaches operating at different times, even within one board meeting. This blend of different approaches partly explains the complexity of the way boards work: the difficulty of holding to account without destroying the levels of trust necessary to allow collaborative stewardship; the need to focus on current operational delivery while developing a sustainable, long-term future.

The implication is that the board needs to have a range of different kinds of conversations, with various areas of focus, and styles, in order to discharge all its responsibilities. Where boards used to spend most of their time on conversations to scrutinize immediate or short-term internal actions, they must now balance that with a broader and longer-term performance focus in addition.

In some sectors, the shift to a purpose-led boardroom is under way, with regulators looking for a clear statement of purpose and evidence that it is made real inside the organization, as described in *Conversation 5: About the organization*. Board members are expected to talk about the organization's role in, and contribution to, society in its widest sense, with an increasing emphasis on sustainability and inclusion.

Figure 2.2 illustrates how these three different *conversational modes* play out in board discussions, in what board members talk about and what they do.

As Figure 2.2 underlines, these modes are additive: boards must be able to operate in all three modes at different times. Sometimes board members will be checking progress against plans, and at other times, perhaps even in the same meeting, reshaping some of those plans in response to an external change.

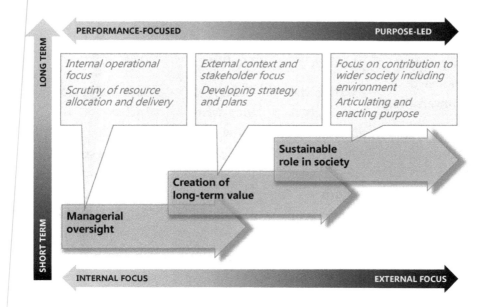

Figure 2.2   Areas of focus and board activities

How this happens is different in every boardroom: the time spent in each of the three modes will vary by organization, sector and as a consequence of current events. For example, if the organization has financial issues, the board may spend most of its time focused on oversight and scrutiny until those problems are solved. But if your board never moves out of the managerial oversight mode, the organization is likely to be missing the benefits of a wider purpose focus.

This is a complicated mix and the sooner you can diagnose what is happening in the conversations round your boardroom table, the sooner you will be able to contribute effectively. Table 2.1 describes the three different modes of board working more clearly, so that you can use it to observe the different kinds of board conversations you and your colleagues have, given what you are trying to achieve. It is a diagnostic tool to help you to take the right conversational approach for each of the tasks that the board must accomplish.

Table 2.1　Modes of board working

Aspects of board conversations	Mode A Managerial oversight	Mode B Creator of long-term value	Mode C Sustainable role in Society
Focus	Delivering shareholder return	Responding to stakeholder needs	Solving a societal issue to create value
Addressing	Information asymmetry	Unlocking value	Defining unique contribution
Role of the board member	Conforming	Performing	Integrating
Board style	Procedural	Collaborative	Explorative
KPIs and metrics	Profit	CSR*	ESG** Moving to SDG***
With the CEO	Checking	Challenging	Coaching
Board dynamics	Structured, and questioning	Contributing and strategizing	Co-creating
Underpinning theory	Agency	Stakeholder	Stewardship

* Corporate Social Responsibility

** Environmental, Social and Governance

*** Sustainable Development Goals

In Mode A, the board's focus is on compliance and conformance. Conversations will be about progress checking, profit or surplus, and centred on fact-finding and explanation as part of the scrutiny role. This is made more difficult by the fact that executives in the organization will always know more than the independent board members; this 'information asymmetry' problem is covered in more detail in *Conversation 8: About holding to account*. The job of the independent board members in this mode is to ensure that they oversee the real issues, despite this problem. But these conversations cannot simply be the test-and-check routines of scrutiny – board members are not operating as examiners, but more as performance coaches, because of their newer and wider responsibilities for longer-term value creation.

In Mode B, the focus of the board goes beyond short-term shareholder return to consider the views of stakeholders, as well as longer-term performance. The board may spend time collaborating on the development of strategy, challenging and supporting executives. In this mode, the organization's sense of its wider role may be expressed in its corporate social responsibility (CSR) activities, perhaps through a range of volunteering and community projects. The evidence suggests that these may often not be fully integrated as part of the organization's strategy, but limited and reactive in nature, and board members will want to explore that problem – which leads the board into the third conversational mode.[18]

In Mode C, the board and the organization will use their statement of purpose to prioritize and make decisions. Conversations will be about exploring societal issues that the organization may be uniquely able to address, moving beyond the sharp focus of CSR and ESG initiatives, which are sometimes viewed as too constrained and limiting. Some organizations use the Sustainable Development Goals (SDGs) set out at the UN Summit in 2015 as a framework for their organization to understand and to engage with 21st-century challenges. Unilever is one such organization, describing the 17 SDGs as an *action plan for the planet and society to thrive by 2030* and using them in their work and their partnerships with others.

Conversation in context

As a board member, particularly as an independent board member, you will need to understand how your board works, because this shapes the leverage and influence you have, as well as the pressures you face.

This context is a function of several factors, including ownership, legal organization structures and the distribution of power round the boardroom table. The better your understanding of this, the more effective you will be as a board member.

Table 2.2 is a simple diagnostic framework to help you to read your situation.

Table 2.2   Understanding your board

Governance question	Options	Why these matter
What is the ownership structure?	Investors, government, partners, employees, families.	The board will have a particular relationship with the owners of the business – this can be complicated if the owners are employed in the business, as for example in a partnership or a family firm.
Who is the board accountable to?	Regulator, government, investors, Charity Commission.	Understanding who and how you are accountable to is vital – is the board signed up to a particular licence arrangement for example?
How is the organization/board regulated?	Name of regulator(s) and area of focus.	You need to know your specific obligations as an independent board member and the legal framework within which the organization works.

Governance question	Options	Why these matter
Who chairs the board?	For example, independent chair, CEO, government minister, civil servant?	It is usual for the board to be chaired by an independent person – it can be another constraint on the functioning of the board if it reports in to the most senior executive (CEO). This duality of function is not encouraged at all in the corporate sector.
Who is on the board?	Independent members, CEO, executives, stakeholder representatives?	Large boards with multiple representatives can result in a diffusion of responsibility where no one feels sufficiently accountable.
Is there a job description for the independent board member?		Beware the 'fig leaf' director, where your main role is to provide respectability to the executive.
What is the balance of the board's work on oversight, strategy and compliance?		The diagnostics of the three conversational modes set out above will help here.
How is the interaction with the executive team managed?	In board meetings, through the CEO only, face-to-face outside meetings?	Some CEOs prevent directors from meeting senior management outside board meetings – this should be a cause for concern.

Governance question	Options	Why these matter
How is stakeholder engagement managed?	By employees and reported to the board, with board members involved, through a specific function, wide involvement?	Stakeholder engagement is increasingly a feature of boards – you should be concerned if this does not appear to take place at board level.

Case study: Triodos Bank purpose statement

This is an example of a purpose statement for an organization, which contains the three elements that will allow it to be enacted inside the organization, and used in setting priorities, allocating resources and making decisions:

Triodos Bank wants to promote human dignity, environmental conservation and a focus on people's quality of life in general. Key to this is a genuinely responsible approach to business, transparency and using money more consciously. Triodos Bank puts values-based banking into practice. We want to connect depositors and investors with socially responsible businesses to build a movement for a more sustainable, socially inclusive society, built on the conscious use of money.[19]

This statement of purpose sets out what the organization does – '*... puts values-based banking into practice*' focusing on the conscious use of money. It describes who its products and services are for – depositors and investors who want to use their money consciously, as well as socially responsible businesses who want investment. It also sets out why, the key third aspect of any purpose statement: '*... promoting human dignity, environmental conservation and a focus on people's quality of life... to build a movement for a more sustainable, socially inclusive society...*'. The conversations round the boardroom table will be shaped by this statement, and the board's choices about what the organization does and how it operates will be driven by it.

Summary

- The idea of what a board is *for* shapes the way it operates – and these ideas have changed over time.
- Agency theory drives a focus on compliance and maximizing returns, while a stakeholder approach requires the board to consider all its stakeholders, not simply the shareholders. Stewardship theory assumes that board members and managers will work together in the service of long-term, sustainable performance.
- In almost every sector, the remit of the board has become broader, with regulators requiring board members to take all three approaches simultaneously – supervising, attending to stakeholders, and serving as stewards.
- This means that the board must operate in different modes, having different sorts of conversations round the boardroom table and outside. Although the blend may vary depending on specific circumstances, this is the conversational challenge: having conversations which hold to account, without destroying the levels of trust necessary to allow collaborative stewardship.
- Understanding your board's context is necessary in responding to this challenge: for example, who owns the organization, who the board is accountable to, how it is regulated and who the board members are, what they talk about, and how they interact with executives.

Checklist: Questions for reflection for board members

Question
Do I have time and capacity to discharge this role, given the increased responsibilities of independent directors?
Am I clear about the role as a board member? (For example, some board roles involve exacting legal responsibilities, while others will require you to act as more of a business adviser.)
Does the board work effectively in the different modes to discharge its particular remit?
Does the board balance the time spent in all three modes appropriately, given the circumstances? For example, is there too much focus on managerial oversight with too little time spent on its broadest stewardship role?

About chairing:
Discussions that matter
to all board members

The chair makes a vital difference to any board – as leader of it, as a member of it – for good or ill. In many ways, the word 'chair' is less a job title and more a job description, not so much a noun but a verb, because what the chair does – and how they do it – is so significant.

So, here the focus is on chairing, the activity that the chair of the board is responsible for, but which board members are involved in and need to understand.

The chair's role

There are many definitions of the chair's role, set out in law and in regulatory guidance, but it is useful to remember that, in summary, *'the chair is the board's boss, not the company's boss'*.[20] Of course, the chair has real influence on the organization, through the board and the working relationship with the CEO, but doesn't run it day to day. This is an important boundary issue, and central in a good working relationship between the two of them.

Given their responsibility for the overall performance of the board, the chair must attend to:

- **Structure:** Taking care to ensure that there is a sound architecture of the governance underpinning the board's work, including committee terms of reference, schedules of delegation and of meetings, as well as reporting lines.
- **Process:** Overseeing, approving and making key decisions, covering both current operations and future plans.
- **Content:** Setting an agenda reflecting the organization's needs and ambitions, which is appropriately strategic and comprehensive, covering both future possibilities as well as present operational realities.

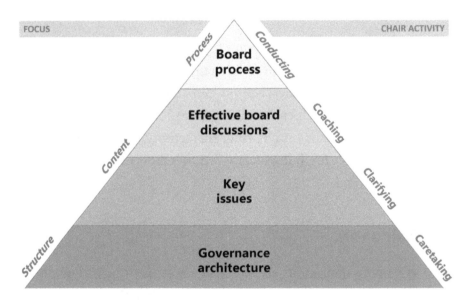

Figure 3.1   Chairing activities

That's *what* the chair does, but *how* they do it sets the tone and style for the board. The chair's behaviour affects how the board contributes – and, in turn, the way that a board talks has a significant effect on the organization and its culture. That will be visible as board members arrive, either ready for a robust and engaging discussion or gloomily awaiting a run-though of the standard agenda, with the usual set of monologues. Stories about what happens in board meetings always leak out into the organization and people learn from them. For example, if the chair regularly keeps people waiting outside the boardroom as the conversation inside overruns, the organization may interpret that as a lack of respect for executives' time, and that will colour attitudes towards the board.

Creating a high-performing board is a complex task, and styles vary. But a good board chair will find themselves working on four activities: caretaking, clarifying, coaching and conducting. Figure 3.1 illustrates how these four combine.

Caretaking

The chair has direct responsibility for the governance framework that the board uses to fulfil its functions. Most organizations operate within a framework set by someone else – for example, company law, or Charity Commission rules, but the chair has to make those require-ments workable in their context. For example, the chair will define committee structures or terms of reference, schedules of delegation, or decide when a short-term working group is needed.

But if the context changes, the chair may need to re-design structures and processes. For example, during the first weeks of the COVID-19 pandemic, many chairs instituted shorter, more frequent, virtual board meetings to help their organization cope. Meetings became more informal – more conversational and less structured – because of the fluidity of the circumstances. The chair has to balance the need to adapt the way the board works, while taking care that such changes are still legally compliant and meet the governance need.

Although structures set the context, it's the board conversations that do the work of governance. That's why the other layers of this model are so important: the chair's responsibility to attend to both the content and the process of the conversations at every meeting and in every interaction both inside and outside the boardroom.

Clarifying

One of the interviewees for this book noted that: '*The real job is getting the right people to talk civilly about the right topics*'. This is harder than it sounds, but it sums up the chair's role. They are involved in recruiting the right people, and must focus the board on what really matters, at the right level of detail, and in an appropriate style.

Good chairs have a clear sense of the rhythm of the board's year and a view of where the organization will be at the end of it. They see the scale of the organization's ambition, and steer through a mix of planned strategic topics, urgent issues and the regular routines of oversight. One chair uses the metaphor of a series of aeroplanes to describe this: at any one point, there will be a large strategic issue on the runway, ready to take off, one in the hangar warming up, plus two in the air, ready to land – and sometimes the runway will need to be cleared for something urgent to be dealt with. The chair needs to have their radar running constantly to clarify for the board over the year what needs attention and when.

A good board conversation really begins before the meeting, and ends after it. The preparation and selection of agenda items, and their timing, is one of the most important sets of decisions that chairs make. The key items on the agenda are the strategic, future-focused conversations, which only the board can have. They require time: if most of the meeting is taken up with reports on current activities, those vital discussion items will be rushed through. And many meeting agendas are clogged up with too many 'for information' items, which could be handled differently – for example, through virtual reviews, off-line briefings, or as shared documents for collective comment.

At the start of a board meeting, good chairs clarify for board members what the meeting will cover and why: highlighting areas where board discussion will be most needed, listing the key decisions to be taken, and reminding the board what's been done since the previous meeting. This sets the tone for the meeting and focuses the discussion.

Coaching

Increasingly, in 21st-century boardrooms, chairs need to use a coaching approach, given their responsibility for the board's collective performance. They may initiate individual or collective conversations, informally or formally, and have a key role in the board's own review of its effectiveness.

Working with individual board members

Getting the best from board members is not simply a matter of annual performance discussions. The chair may need to initiate a private conversation with a particular board member about their contribution during the meeting. This might be positive reinforcement: *'Thank you for your interjection at today's meeting – it made a real difference to the discussion, and to the outcome'.* Alternatively, it might be a conversation where a change is needed: *'Do you feel that your point was heard in today's meeting? Shall we talk about how we might get more value from your contributions?'* Contribution is a function both of what is said and whether it is heard, and the chair's role is to ensure that every member of the board is able to contribute effectively.

Conversations with the CEO

The working relationship between the chair and the CEO is critical to the board's performance: it needs to be close enough for honesty on both sides, but not cosy. This implies that there will be a blend of challenge and support in their conversations. It's a complex relationship: for example, the chair may well contribute to the CEO's performance appraisal (see *Conversation 11: With the CEO*), but will also operate as a clear-eyed, critical friend, drawing on their own experience to help the CEO to perform effectively.

Recent studies suggest that conversations between the chair and the CEO or the most senior leader have become more informal, shorter but more frequent, and often occur virtually, a trend that was accelerated during the COVID-19 pandemic.[21] Although chairs often have extensive experience to contribute as a mentor, increasingly, they will move into coaching mode, too, helping the CEO to reflect on their own performance.

Board performance coaching

The chair serves as a coach for the board as a whole during formal effectiveness reviews – and there is much more about these important conversations in *Conversation 10: About effectiveness.* This process is a collective reflection on how the board operates and it may include discussions with individuals about their contribution and development needs.

The chair can help the board to develop its own boardroom etiquette, making explicit how they want to work together. Some boards actively define their own conversational rituals, as part of this. For example, one board agreed on four principles for their interactions: they wanted their discussions to be *courteous, collegiate, constructive* and *clear.* The chair then acted as a coach, helping them to follow their own agreed rules.

Conducting

Chairing is a complex leadership activity, different from that of a senior leader with direct, executive responsibility. The chair literally conducts the board's work and its meetings through all four of these activities: taking care of its governance structures, focusing the board on key issues, creating the conditions for effective board discussions and running a boardroom process.

The chair's role is rather like that of an orchestral conductor: choosing an appropriate programme given the abilities of the musicians, setting the tempo and the mood for the performance, bringing in different players at different times, guiding the ensemble if the performance goes off track. He or she stands visibly at the apex of power, in front of all the musicians. But an orchestral conductor is the only person on the stage who is not making any sound themselves. Their contribution is to energize and bring together the group of specialist musicians in harmony – and there's the parallel with the way effective chairs operate.

Conducting board meetings

Board meetings demonstrate this point. The chair will have set the agenda, and will, of course, contribute their views but must orchestrate the contribution of all board members. Chairs who dominate discussions turn the collective orchestral performance into a solo with accompaniment, and the board's oversight will suffer as a result. Many codes of practice specifically warn of the dangers of any one individual having unfettered power. So, the guidance for chairs in expressing their own views might be summed up as, 'say it, but be careful how you say it', as one chair put it.

The pyramid model underlines the point: the chair must manage both the *process* of the conversation, as well as simultaneously attending to its *content*. This twin focus brings some dilemmas with it: the need to steer the conversation, but to listen more than talk; to encourage all board members to contribute if they wish to, but still manage the time effectively; to contribute but to avoid anchoring the board's discussions with too dominant or too frequent statements of their own views.

The chair is responsible for some basic conversational processes: to summarize what has been said during the meeting fully and clearly, including views with which they don't agree, and to ensure that decisions and actions are captured in the record of the meeting, for example. The chair uses the governance framework to move conversations to a more appropriate mode where necessary, synchronous or asynchronous. If, for example, challenge from board directors becomes prolonged, the chair may need to move the discussion off-line.

But the chair also needs to monitor the content of what is said, ensuring that the discussion is at an appropriate level of detail for the topic. It is the chair's job to pull the conversation out of the weeds if necessary.

Conducting different kinds of conversation

Boards work in different modes, given the range of their responsibilities, as described in *Conversation 2: About the board*. For example, managerial oversight (Mode A working) tends to be procedural, with a focus on structured questioning, while when the board is more focused on the creation of long-term value and stakeholder needs (Mode B working), their style of conversation will tend to be more collaborative. When they are working in Mode C, the board will spend time exploring the nature of the long-term external problem rather than planning how to implement solutions.

To be effective the board will need to switch conversational modes, even during a single board meeting, and it is the chair's job to help them to do that.

Case study: Clearing the air

One chair working with a combined board of executives and non-executives noticed the lack of mutual understanding about priorities and workload around the boardroom table. That made discussions more acrimonious than effective. Before the next board meeting, the chair took the opportunity to talk to the CEO about this:

'I do understand that you have about a thousand things to do but I need to tell you that the non-execs on the board think that you

have only two things to do – the two things they told you to do at the
last meeting. Neither of you are wrong. It is my job as chair to trans-
late between these two worlds, to act as a bridge. And I'll be having
this conversation with them, too, to put your perspective across'.

That preparatory conversation was sufficient to unblock the
log-jam of misunderstanding. It didn't by itself solve the problem
of different perceptions of priorities, but it laid the groundwork for
a more constructive conversation.

In this example, the chair was clarifying a problem for both the
CEO and the non-executives and generating a coaching conversation to resolve it.

Summary

- The word 'chair' is more a verb than a noun, describing a
  complex activity that makes a critical difference to the board's
  performance.
- The chair leads the board but is not the direct leader of the
  organization. They have real influence but they don't run the
  business.
- The responsibility for the performance of the board requires
  them to attend to structures, processes and content, and the
  way in which they do so sets the style and tone for the board.
- Leading a high performing board requires four activities in
  particular:
  - *Caretaking* the architecture of governance within the orga-
    nization's legal framework;
  - *Clarifying* what matters over the board's year, areas of focus,
    key issues and how they are best addressed;

◻ *Coaching*, to ensure that the board collectively performs its governance role and that all individual members are able to contribute effectively in their different roles;

◻ *Conducting*, orchestrating board member contributions and the different conversational modes required.

Checklist: Questions for reflection for the chair

Activity	Focus	Questions for reflection
Caretaking	On the governance architecture for the board and the organization.	Does the architecture meet our legal requirements as well as the organization's particular needs? If not, what can we do about it, while remaining compliant?
		Are the roles and structures within the architecture clear to the board and to those who serve in those roles? For example, audit committee chair, remuneration committee scope?
		Is the architecture clearly documented so that new board members can understand it?
		Is it always clear what topics go where in our structure – to the board, to committees, to working groups, or to the executive?
		Has the context changed so that some of our structures and processes also need to change (e.g., for virtual working)?
		Do we have good board secretariat support, people who understand the structure and can help the board work effectively within it?
		Do we make appropriate use of off-line meetings, working groups, asynchronous reviews of papers?

Activity	Focus	Questions for reflection
Clarifying	The key issues for the board as a whole.	What are the top strategic issues for the organization which need to be addressed this year? What are we doing about them – which issues are 'on the runway', and which need to be 'landed' by the end of the year?
	Board meeting processes.	Does the agenda reflect the key issues, as well as the regular reports for oversight? Is there sufficient time for discussion?
		Do I start each meeting with a clear statement about the focus of the meeting and the key decisions to be made during it?
		Are decisions made and recorded clearly, with the rationale documented too?
		Do I summarize the board's views at the end of each discussion, including those views that I don't agree with?
	The concerns of particular sub-groups within the board – e.g., the executive or independent board members.	Do board members understand each other's priorities? Is there space for a conversation to help them to understand?
		What do we do when the board is divided and takes irreconcilable views on an issue? For example, is there an explicit process for voting or restarting the conversation at another time?
Coaching	Board performance	Do we have regular reviews of the board's performance – at the end of a meeting, as well as annually or bi-annually?
		Do board members have individual objectives or areas of focus each year?
	Individual contributions	Do I have the opportunity to talk to individuals about their contribution to the board? Do these conversations make a difference to performance?

Activity	Focus	Questions for reflection
		Do I identify development activity for individual members and does this happen? Does it make a difference to their contribution?
	CEO performance	Do I have regular discussions with the CEO, not simply before a board meeting? Do these meetings have a set agenda, or do they reflect current issues, whatever they may be?
		Do I have a sense that the CEO benefits from these conversations? Do actions arise and are they done?
		Am I able to challenge the CEO? Do I provide appropriate support, too?
		Do I contribute to the CEO's performance appraisal, or undertake it directly?
		How would I describe my relationship with the CEO?
Conducting	Using the board's resources well.	Are appropriate resources devoted to the key strategic issues, both from the board and from the organization?
		Does the board respond to new issues that might suddenly arise – for example, does the agenda change? Is it possible to call additional meetings if necessary? Can I work virtually or resolve an issue off-line if necessary?
		Is it clear to board members when the board conversation needs to be in a different mode – for example, managerial oversight or strategy discussions? Is there sufficient time for these various conversations?

With board members:
Sense-checking conversations

Board oversight is a collective responsibility that board members discharge together, particularly in conversations round the boardroom table. But conversations *outside* the boardroom are necessary for a variety of reasons: to clarify the information presented to the board; to deal with complex issues when there simply isn't sufficient time in the board meeting; and to get the benefit of the varied experience of board members.

However, these off-line conversations between board members, although vital, may come at a price, as explored here. This is the challenge for the chair, and for all board members: to ensure that these valuable off-line conversations are still productive for the board as a whole – that they deliver more upside than downside.

An effective working group

Boards are like a Rubik's Cube of members with different skills, experiences and styles; each plays particular roles in the organization and has different affiliations to it. That's one of the reasons why board dynamics are so complex. Board members have a shared purpose, and equal and shared accountability for their collective task – to oversee the work of the organization – but some members of the board will also work for other organizations in different capacities. The board as a whole spends less time together than an executive management team, partly because the role is to govern not to manage.[22] So, the board is not a single team in the traditional sense, but it must function as an effective work group.[23]

Sub-group dynamics

The diversity of board member roles and experiences creates sub-groups within most boards. The conversations within and between those sub-groups, often off-line and outside the boardroom, are surprisingly important in exercising collective governance.

The internal affiliations inside each sub-group help it to function. For example, the strength of the working relationship between the chair and the CEO is a key ingredient in the board's work, as discussed in *Conversation 3: About chairing.* Executive members of the board form another sub-group with their greater knowledge and responsibility for implementation. The board's committees operate as sub-groups, made up of board members with particular expertise, working on specific aspects such as audit or remuneration. The independent board members share the specific challenge of exercising oversight with limited information and time, and they bring in external experience.

Effective boards operate by bringing together the different views and disparate approaches of these sub-groups to their collective task. The board's success is not measured by the degree of compliance and similarity of their views, but by the way they are collectively able to use their diversity to best effect.

The benefits of off-line conversations

Collective sense-making in a complex world is no easy task. Informal conversations, outside the meeting, with other colleagues are vital – in building mutual understanding, laying the foundations for good working relationships, exploring differences of view and sometimes resolving issues before they dominate and distract the whole board.

Boards typically receive considerable amounts of data about the work of the organization, but their papers obviously don't tell them every single thing that is happening and why. (Or at least, they shouldn't.) The task of prioritizing, therefore, or spotting the smaller issues that could derail the operation is never easy and is better done in collaboration. Independent board members in particular benefit from some off-line sense-checking, or clarification on board papers with executive members of the board.

These side conversations are mostly about exploring issues, not pre-empting the board's discussion. They create a conversational space to compare reactions to an issue – for example: *'This seems more risky to me than the paper suggests – how do you see it?'* Some board members may have seen a similar situation in the past and have insight to offer. Others may simply have a nagging intuition that all is not well, and want to test their assessment. These conversations allow time to notice the weak signals of a possible problem, which may be missed in long board meetings.

They are also the chance for board members to reflect on the agenda as a whole: Are we talking about the right things? What topics are we not talking about, ones that never seem to be on the meeting agenda? Agenda setting is a key responsibility of the chair, as discussed in *Conversation 3: About chairing*, but since board members share the collective responsibility for oversight, they will want to contribute views.

Disadvantages

Although extremely valuable, off-line interactions can create difficulties. They can appear to be secretive conversations, breeding a sense of them-and-us between different sub-groups of board members. For example, side-conversations between independent board members tend to make executives nervous, because it is not clear to them what is being discussed, or why. You can see this when, for example, boards of trustees schedule private time at the end of a meeting and the executive members of the board leave the room, visibly apprehensive.

Off-line discussions may exacerbate the problem of different levels of understanding: those who have had the off-line conversation know more than those who have not, making constructive conversation round the table harder. It may even feel like board meetings have two agendas: the published agenda and a hidden agenda developed by a sub-group. And such discussions may get out of hand, generating extra work for executives or the board secretary team, or creating disproportionate alarm about a particular topic. Finally, new members may find it difficult to get involved if there is a long-standing pattern of informal off-line conversations.

Effective choreography for off-line conversations

The chair of the board will certainly be watching for these downsides and will want to work with the board to minimize them.

One of the ways to manage these informal off-line conversations is to make them more formal and visible, and, at times, extend an open invitation to others to join. Scheduling sub-group conversations overtly reminds the whole board that these conversations help them to perform their board role. Off-line discussions between independent board members and the chair, for example, are increasingly seen as part of good governance and the UK Corporate Governance Code requires them.[24]

Clarification conversations

Many boards set up a regular forum for members in advance of the board meeting, simply to ask questions of clarification about topics on the board's agenda. Board members may ask about the coherence and reliability of the information provided, or whether it is consistent with other information which they have seen. These conversations help board meetings to be more focused and purposeful, and can be particularly useful for those organizations which hold open board meetings.

Sometimes this generates requests for more information about a particular topic, in preparation for the boardroom discussion. But board members need to calibrate their demands in line with the significance of the topic and the capacity of the organization to respond effectively. More information and more detail will not always help the board to perform its role effectively.

Offering feedback

Some form of feedback from these off-line interactions is important, and can help to allay anxieties. For example, the chair might choose to let the CEO know what is likely to be covered in private discussions with independent board members, even though there may not be a formal agenda. Providing some feedback after the conversation helps, too, although there is a balance to be struck here: these particular conversations shouldn't be too tightly structured or reported since they are intended to be a forum for reflection, for advice to the chair and for sense-checking.

Regulating the conversations

Independent members should also take care to manage the emotional temperature of their off-line conversations. Reflections on a difficult board meeting sometimes generate more heat than light, and that should not spill over into the board as a whole. If the sense-checking process reveals that many board members are concerned about particular issues, the conversation might generate a disproportionate collective reaction – groupthink – which raises executive hackles and doesn't help to generate an appropriate response. One interviewee talked about the 'death spiral' of such conversations – recognizing the problem, but constantly circling round a range of possible solutions, unable to find an outcome in this sub-group conversation.

Scheduling face-to-face discussions

Finally, it's worth holding these sub-group conversations in person, if at all possible. It makes them both more visible to other members of the board and more effective. Sense-checking is a conversational process that requires board members to learn from each other, listening attentively and observing body language, so that they can collectively calibrate the significance of a given topic. This is much harder to do when working virtually, as both research and anecdotal experience indicate.

Case study: A question of approach

The paper before the board was a simple request for approval for funding: the organization intended to create a new advisory board made up of key stakeholders and needed funding for a small team to support this new board.

The request had come to the board because the financial investment for the team was outside delegated limits – it was not intended to be a discussion of the decision to create a new advisory board.

But the independent board members had spent many previous meetings discussing the actions and concerns of this stakeholder group. As a result, in their off-line discussions before the board meeting, they felt strongly that the agenda item asked the wrong question: not about whether there should be a small team to support a new advisory board, but whether such a board should be established at all.

At the meeting, the independent board members expressed their views bluntly. Members of the executive were furious, feeling ambushed and undermined. The subsequent decision not to proceed with the proposal may have been the right one, but the mode of making the decision damaged working relationships within the board.

The independent members subsequently recognized that it would have been better to discuss their collective view with senior management before the meeting. That approach would have allowed the right decision to be made while still preserving working relationships.

Summary

- Conversation is key in getting the best from the diverse skills, styles and experiences of board members, and some of these conversations need to happen off-line and outside the boardroom.
- Boards are not typically a team in the traditional sense, but they need to be an effective work group, with a series of sub-groups.
- Sub-group conversations are an important part of sense-checking and forming appropriate, measured judgements as a board.
- But there are downsides to these conversations, which have to be managed through careful choreography: overt scheduling, providing feedback, regulating the emotional temperature and, where possible, meeting in person.

Checklist: Talking with board colleagues

Off-line conversations with:	Focus	Questions to cover
Fellow independent board members	Sense-checking understanding	How do you see this issue? How do you assess the level of risk in this proposal? Have you seen anything like this before and what happened in that situation?
		Are you satisfied that this information is accurate and complete?
	Exploring significance	Do you see this as a red flag, signalling an approaching problem? Might this issue/proposal interact with other issues facing the organization – combining to make the problem worse?

Off-line conversations with:	Focus	Questions to cover
	Checking oversight	What are we not talking about? What is not on the agenda? How do we oversee that issue/aspect (e.g., in a committee)?
	The feedback loop	What sort of feedback from this conversation, if any, should we provide and to whom? Do we need to talk about this issue as a board and, if so, when?
Executive board members	Clarification of content, coherence and consistency of data	Questions to understand board papers: for example, about the source of the data, the level and type of analysis, options considered but rejected. Is this information coherent? Does this information make sense in the light of other data which the board has seen – is it consistent?
The chair	Key issues for the board	What are you as chair currently most concerned about?
		How do we feel that the last board meeting went?
		What do we want to focus on at our next board meeting?
		How and where do we oversee the topics which are not on the board's agenda?

About the organization: Talking about purpose, mission, vision and values

To be an effective board member, you must know what this organization is for, what it does and how it does it, for whom and with whom. Your induction conversations are the opportunity to learn about the organization and also to build working relationships. You may already be familiar with some aspects, but your role is to consider what is best for the organization as a whole, not just for the part of it you understand best.

So, don't miss the window of opportunity to understand the organization's purpose, strategy and values, the basic business model, and its context. You will also want to learn more about the board itself, of course, and there is more about that in *Conversation 2: About the board*.

Ethnography for new board members

During your induction, you might think of yourself as an ethnographer, a technique introduced earlier in this book: someone who learns about the organization's structures, systems and people by observing without judgement from inside. You will have some initial ideas from the research you did as part of the application process, so this is a chance to compare the reality with what you have read.

This is the perfect time to ask the basic but necessary questions, because you are not, yet, expected to know about the business. You have licence to talk to members of staff who interact with customers, or the teams who do some of the key tasks in the business. Don't leave it too late: there are questions you can ask in the first few weeks that might be embarrassing to ask after a few months. These conversations will probably be at a more detailed level than you will need as a board member, but they will help you make sense of the view from 30,000 feet.

Your induction programme should be planned to reflect what you already know and what you don't, and there is plenty of guidance about what to cover in these first few weeks.[25] Regulators in most sectors emphasize the importance of these early conversations and they will help you to become effective quickly.

Purpose, mission, vision and values

The work of a board should be grounded on an organization's statement of purpose, vision, mission and values. These documents set out what the organization says about itself, and give you a basis on which to examine the reality. But they can often be confused: the UK Financial Reporting Council notes that some companies conflate vision and mission with purpose, for example.[26]

This set of definitions clarifies what each statement is for:

- a purpose statement articulates *why* an organization exists;
- a mission statement sets out *what* the organization does;
- a vision statement describes *where* the organization intends to have impact – the outcome that it wants to see from successful delivery of its purpose;
- a values statement articulates *how* the organization behaves.

The purpose statement is central – and often the one that is missing. It should be a lodestone for the board, guiding the organization, and the source of the vision and mission statements, as well as the strategy. In some organizations, it's easy to find: if you are joining the board of a charity, look at the charity deed for a statement of its purpose, objectives and the scope of its work. If the organization doesn't have a purpose statement, that will be a task for the board, since this is increasingly regarded as best practice in many sectors.

In some sectors, such statements are also now required: for example, the UK's Corporate Governance Code of 2018 emphasizes that boards should define and articulate the company's purpose and values, along with its strategy. This is because they are useful: they should contain a set of principles the board can use in prioritizing and making decisions. To be most effective, purpose statements need to contain three elements: a reference to the problem that the organization aims to solve, a definition of customers or service users, and a statement about the scope of operations in terms of product, service or geography.

Alignment

Best practice also suggests that this set of statements – purpose, vision, mission and values – should be coherent and aligned with each other. They don't each have to be perfectly crafted, but you should be able to see a logical connection between them, because they should all be derived from the statement of purpose. This is what it means to be 'purpose-led', as described in *Conversation 2: About the board*.

Matching reality

During your induction, compare what you read in these statements with what you observe: do they match the reality inside the organization? Are they used when difficult decisions need to be made?

If the statement of the organization's values is to be more than a set of words on a website, you should be able to see it in your conversations with members of staff. Observing your board colleagues at your first few board meetings will also be informative. How do people talk to each other in the meetings and how, in particular, do they deal with differences of opinion? These value statements are part of the culture – and observing and understanding the organization's culture is one of the key techniques in your kitbag, as discussed in the Introduction.

Conversations to understand constitutions and regulators

Board members have a duty to the legal entity – whether that is a company, trust, public body, or partnership – so you need to understand the framework within which the organization operates. Read the legal underpinnings of this organization – for example, its charter, trust deed or articles of association. *Conversation 2: About the board* offers a diagnostic tool to help you to understand how your board works within its framework.

Ask about regulation: who regulates organizations in this sector and how? For example, charitable trusts must report regularly to the Charity Commission and declare any serious incidents that have occurred. School regulation operates through inspections, which require governors or trustees to be involved. *Conversation 14: With regulators* has more to say about this important topic, but, at the induction stage, start with a briefing conversation, and then read recent reports on this organization from the regulator.

This organization's journey

If you are charged with board responsibility for building the future, it helps to know what's happened in the past. How did this organization get to this point in its development? This is an excellent topic for your conversations with staff: get them to tell you the story of this organization's journey as they see it. What are the key events, crises or changes that have occurred while they have been working here?

These conversations will help you to understand what has been tried in the past, and whether it worked or not. Organizations typically have what might be called 'scar tissue' from previous initiatives or changes, which may generate resistance to new changes. Understanding this at the outset will help you and the board make realistic plans for the future.

Business model

Board members must understand the basics of the organization: where the money comes from and is spent, who its customers are and what it does for them. Some board members may feel that this is too detailed a viewpoint if the board is supposed to operate at the strategic level, but strategic thinking must be grounded in reality.

Your preparatory reading will help you with this, but conversations with members of staff who actually do the work of the organization will be worth your time. Talk to a teacher during morning break in a school, or visit a branch operation or a satellite office to meet people who work there. And if you can invest the time, ask to spend an hour or two sitting alongside staff and get them to tell you about the systems they use, what kinds of issues they face and what they would change if they could. Of course, you will hear their personal views, but it will help you to bring alive what you read in board papers.

Creating value

Board members should ask themselves the question: *Where do we create value and for whom?* Understanding this is vital: it allows the board to steer 'strategies and business models towards a sustainable future'.[27]

Value might be defined in different ways – financial, provision of services, reputation, market share, staff skills, intellectual property, for example – and some of these might be more of a focus at times than others. Some are tangible, and will be visible in the annual report and accounts, while others are intangible; both are central in overseeing the organization's activities.

Market or external context

The board needs awareness of a range of external factors that may affect its plans. Many boards have a tendency to focus on internal matters – a 'centripetal pull', which is not always helpful – and, as an independent board member, you can rebalance the discussions. You may know less about the internal details of the organization than your executive colleagues, but you have the time and the opportunity to learn more about the outside world – and the board needs those insights.

So, in conversations outside the organization, look for the ideas and developments which may be useful to your board – even from different sectors. The PESTEL acronym helps here:

- **Political** developments in the sector may be important. Are there policy changes ahead, or increased regulation, for example?
- **Economically**, what is happening in this market? Is it, for example, growing or shrinking? Who are the main competitors? Are there new competitors coming into this market? Which organizations are no longer competitors and why – have they, for example, become insolvent or moved into new markets?
- **Social** factors also affect this organization – attitudes to its work, or changes in lifestyles which affect how it operates.
- **Technology** is always changing, creating opportunities but also new pressures. Are there new innovations in products or processes which the board should understand as it formulates new strategies?
- **Environmental** changes have already affected organizations and will continue to do so, as both attitudes and regulations change. How is this developing in your sector?

- **Legal** changes in the market may have significant effects – for example, changes in employment law or minimum wage levels.

Too often, boards consider these aspects only at the annual strategy away-day. But, as a new board member, developing your knowledge of what's happening outside the organization gives you something useful to contribute in board conversations.

Case study: Understanding the organization

The board of a company running three nursery schools appointed a new independent member, with many years of experience as a governor of a local primary school. She brought her knowledge of the care and development of children and already understood the non-executive aspect of the board role, so her induction focused purely on the legal responsibilities of being a company director.

But nurseries are run very differently from primary schools: this was an independent business, privately owned, not state-run; it was funded by fees rather than annual grants; it operated over 50 weeks of the year, not to termly schedules; some children attended only part-time; and the level of staff turnover was much higher than in the school sector.

It took time for her to understand these fundamental differ-ences and the effect on the board's work. For example, sudden crises requiring immediate attention had to be dealt with outside board meetings, while the meetings themselves focused much more on operational decisions about money and staffing – fee collection, debt management and recruitment – than in primary schools.

Although both nurseries and schools focus on the care and development of children, she found that the business model is very different, and so the governance responsibilities of board members are also different.

Summary

- Induction conversations are vital in preparing to be an effective board member: understanding what the organization does, why and how is the foundation for contributing to oversight and direction setting.
- Hearing about the organization's purpose, vision, mission and values in conversations with people throughout the organization allows you to observe the reality, to see whether it matches what these statements set out.
- Board members must understand the legal and regulatory framework within which they operate: what their duties are in law, and what the regulator expects from them.
- Talking to staff about the story of the organization's journey is informative; understanding its past helps you to understand and oversee the present, as well as planning for its future.
- Understand the business model of this organization: where the money comes from and is spent, who its customers are and what it does for them. Board members should be able to identify where value is created and for whom.
- Boards need to be aware of external factors that may affect them and it's part of the role of independent board members to contribute such insights.

Checklist: Questions to consider

Topic	Questions to consider – for observation or conversation
Purpose, vision, mission statements	• Do we have a purpose statement that contains three key elements of useful purpose statements: scope, service to customers or users, and the problem we address? • When did we last review it to be sure it serves us in our current context?

Topic	Questions to consider – for observation or conversation
	• How often do we refer to this purpose statement when we have hard decisions to make? • Do we have a vision statement setting out where we intend to be in time? Does this match what we say in our strategic plan? • Are these statements clear to everyone in the organization? • Do people believe them and find them useful?
Values statements	• Do board members behave in line with our values? Does the board display the behaviour we expect from our people? • Do people believe in this statement of what the organization values? Are there examples of where we do live our values, and where we don't? When we recruit, induct, train, promote, appraise or when we terminate an employee's contract? • Do our remuneration systems align with our values – are we actually rewarding what we say we value in how people behave?
Ownership	• Who owns this organization? What is your relationship with them?
The organization's legal constitution	• What's the legal framework within which the organization operates (e.g., its charter, framework document, trust deed, formation articles, memorandum of understanding, articles of association, or legislation, etc.)? • Who regulates organizations in this sector and how?
The organization's journey	• How did the organization get to where it is now – what's the story of its development? Have there been major changes, acquisitions or disposals, changes in products or services? • Have there been crises and, if so, how were they addressed?

Topic	Questions to consider – for observation or conversation
The business model	• Where does our funding come from and where is most of it spent? • Where do we create value and for whom? What do our customers or service users value most about what we offer?

The external context or market	• What's happening externally and how might this affect this organization:
	  ▫ Politically?
	  ▫ Economically?
	  ▫ Socially?
	  ▫ Technologically?
	  ▫ Environmentally?
	  ▫ Legally?

Organization culture	• What can you learn about the culture of this organization, using the culture web (from the *Introduction*)? • Does this culture support the organization in delivering its purpose?

About strategy:
Turning central ideas into action

Strategy conversations are some of the most important that the board will have. They differ from other board conversations: they are future-oriented, less about oversight and more about options, and they require both internal organizational knowledge as well as external insights. Most of all, they should generate a story about the organization's future, and how to get from where they are now to where they want to be.

Talking about strategy

One of the many reasons organizations need strategy is because they have constrained resources, including time: such constraints impose choices on the organization and the board will want to make those choices consciously. That's the point of the conversation.

In the past, some boards would simply approve a strategy developed inside the organization, as an exercise in managerial oversight (working in Mode A, as described in *Conversation 2: About the board*). Now most boards discharge their responsibility for strategy through collaborative conversations round the boardroom table, and with stakeholders (working in Mode B, as set out in *Conversation 2: About the board*). And because implementation is the responsibility of executive leaders, they too must be part of this conversation. Their greater knowledge of what the organization is capable of is vital in defining an achievable strategy.

Effective strategy conversations have some particular characteristics, although the specific content will vary according to the context. They require a clear understanding of the present, but they must also address possible future events. Discussion about the future is so important that the next conversation is devoted specifically to the board's responsibilities to look ahead and interpret what might happen. This is an integral part of the strategy conversation, but it is no simple topic, hence the focus on it in *Conversation 7: About the future*. And their conversations will be a blend of facts and ideas, options to consider as well as those to discard, since strategy involves saying no as well as yes.

Throughout these conversations, the board will want to talk about internal and external dimensions: the organization's *purpose* and its *resources*, as well as the *opportunities* available now or that might arise. These three topics are the scaffolding for boardroom strategy conversations, and all three need to be in balance, as Figure 6.1 illustrates.

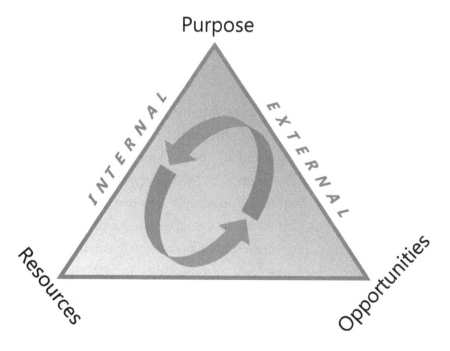

Figure 6.1   Balancing purpose, opportunities and resources

If the conversations focus too much on the internal dimensions, the strategy may prove to be unrealistic because there is too little consideration of the external realities – for example, market changes or competitor activity, which might create new opportunities.

Equally, if the strategy conversation focuses too much on actual or possible opportunities without considering the organization's ability to respond, the strategy may be unfocused and be a recipe for risky diversification. When a new opportunity arises, or the strategy changes, the board must ask whether the organization has the right competences.

In these discussions, board members will want to use a range of different lenses, as described in the *Introduction*, taking a broad scan of their current context ('binoculars') and looking ahead for hidden opportunities or possible future developments ('rose-coloured glasses').

Starting the conversation

The conversation typically starts with a review of some key questions, to be sure they are still valid: why this organization exists (purpose), what it does (mission), where it intends to have impact (vision) and how it intends to operate (values). This is because the strategy task is to set out a realistic route to achieve the organization's purpose, given its context, and in line with its values.

Sometimes, the strategy conversation may start by revising the statement of purpose, or the vision or mission. This is because these statements tend to be a function of the particular stage of the organization's development and its context. As the external world changes, or the organization develops, so the definitions may need to alter.

Focused on purpose

The statement of purpose is increasingly important in organizations: regulators in some sectors expect to see it articulated in the annual report and staff comment that a sense of purpose is a key part of their motivation. *Conversation 5: About the organization* sets out the three key characteristics of sound purpose statements: they define the scope of what the organization does, they make reference to the customer or end user and there is a connection to the problem to be solved. It should be clear what outcome the organization wants to see from successful delivery of its purpose – its vision – and that will drive the strategy work.

Three strategy questions

The strategy conversation usually covers three simple but vital questions:

1. Where are we now?
2. Where do we want to be?
3. How do we get there?

Question 1 will involve a discussion of the organization's present position, both internally and externally. This will involve a review of the organization's resources, financial strength, areas of known weakness, as well as any planned internal changes, such as the scheduled departure of a senior leader or a new system implementation. And, looking externally, to understand the organization's market position, stakeholder relationships and reputation.

Question 2 is typically harder to answer: Where do we want to be, and when, given our purpose, vision and mission? Where is it realistic to aim for? Where are the opportunities for us? This conversation links the internal and external perspectives and may well generate a range of different options.

Question 3 asks the board to consider how the organization might move from the present to its intended future state: What needs to be changed, what developed, what acquired or disposed of? Here the board will set the outlines for more detailed analytical and action planning work to be done subsequently inside the organization.

The strategy process in organizations

Strategy formulation is an iterative process, which happens in the boardroom and outside. It is both bottom-up and top-down; the board's conversations drive strategy work in individual departments or teams, but are also shaped by that more detailed thinking. Many organizations now involve members of staff in these strategy conversations: front-line staff often have useful perspectives to add because they understand the work of the organization and will be involved in the implementation work. Getting staff to 'buy-in' to a strategy handed down from the top of an organization is much less effective than involving them in its creation.

So, the orchestration of the process is vital, and the board will want to talk about this at the outset: who will be involved and how the top-down and bottom-up conversations will connect.

Ideally, the board's conversation will set the parameters at the outset: objectives, timescale and areas of focus. The board may also wish to define those areas which are out of scope. For example, in a consolidating market, the board may specify that over the strategy period they want to grow by expanding their operations in some geographies but not in others. Alternatively, the board may want to exclude any plans to outsource part of the organization's work, or to look for opportunities to do just this.

The outcome

As the work draws to a conclusion, a final draft strategy (probably completed outside the board) is usually brought back to the board for a final discussion, for approval or adjustment. The conversation at this stage should not involve detailed word-smithing of the document, but rather allow time to consider the strategy overall, because it will drive the board's reviews of progress in every board meeting to come. The checklist at the end of this conversation contains an expanded set of questions to help in this sign-off conversation.

The simplest test of all is to ask whether this strategy tells a clear, compelling *story* which looks achievable and is in line with the organization's statements about purpose, vision, mission and values. That story then needs to turn into action – in other words, the strategy needs to turn into a plan. The board will want to see a clear process and timetable for that work.

Reviewing and revising strategy regularly

Although strategy conversations tend to be formally scheduled, perhaps at the annual strategy workshop or away-day, the board needs to be ready to move into strategy mode whenever there is a change, whether in the context or inside the organization. Sometimes, a simple discussion with the executive about what appears to be a minor short-term investment can have strategic implications and therefore require a fuller discussion.

Once the direction has been set, the board needs to keep the compass in its hands, monitoring the outside world, as well as internal activities, to see if their strategy choices need to be re-examined. But the board needs to resist the temptation to tinker constantly with the strategy once it has been agreed. The organization needs to execute it with purpose, and excessive 'What if…?' conversations or changes of direction will prevent it from doing so.

Emergent strategy

This conversation looks at how organizations might generate what business schools call *deliberate* strategy. But in complex and rapidly changing contexts, or where the organization is very new, some boards decide to adopt an *emergent* strategy. They may have a clear purpose and a sense of direction, but choose to take a more flexible approach, seizing new opportunities as they arise, or pursuing internal innovations. If so, the board's strategy conversations will need to be more frequent, based on a wider and deeper knowledge of what is happening in their market. And the organization will need to be designed to be nimble, fostering new ideas, with flexible resources and ready access to investment.

Case study: Transforming purpose and role

Companies House is a government body responsible for capturing and storing information about all limited companies and limited liability partnerships registered in the UK. The UK Economic Crime and Corporate Transparency Bill will fundamentally change its role and purpose, giving it greater powers to play a more significant role in tackling economic crime.

The organization has developed a new purpose statement: *'Driving confidence in the UK economy'*. As a consequence, the strategy for the organization maps a transition from being the home of company information to being an active gatekeeper of the data on its registers, helping to prevent the misuse of corporate entities.

The new strategy for Companies House for 2020–2025 explains the significance of these additional powers:

'We are now on the threshold of major change, recognising that there is much more that we can do to respond to the expectations of our stakeholders and our own aspirations... This will transform not just what we do but how we do it – transforming our services, our culture and our ways of working... We will ensure that legislative changes are translated into new systems and processes that work for our customers, as well as effectively delivering that vision'.[28]

Summary

- Strategy conversations differ from other board conversations: they are purpose-driven, focused on the future, and bring together both the internal analysis of resources as well as a view of the external context.

- They typically start with the fundamentals: why the organization exists (purpose), what the organization does (mission), where it intends to have impact (vision).
- The board's task is to set out a route to achieve its purpose, given the current context. Strategy is about story and it has to make sense, and be achievable.
- The strategy process is iterative, both top-down and bottom-up, with the board setting parameters at the outset and signing it off.
- The three key strategy questions are:
  - First, where are we now?
  - Second, where do we want to be?
  - Third, how do we get there?
- Strategy review is a regular process: having set the direction, boards must keep the compass in their hands to review progress.

Checklist: Strategy review questions

Aspect	Review question
Outcome	Does this strategy achieve our purpose?
	Does it move the organization towards our vision in a realistic timescale?
	Is there a clear story about the direction we are planning to take and what we will (and possibly will not) do? Can we explain our strategy and how we and our stakeholders and customers derive value from it?
	How does it differentiate us from our closest competitors?
	How consistent is this strategy with our values?
External context	What assumptions have we made about the external world/ the market and are they explicit and reasonable?
	Are there market opportunities which this strategy misses – or that we are excessively focused on?

Aspect	Review question
Process	Did the board set the parameters for the strategy, including what is out of scope as well as the areas to be explored?
	Have we involved the right people in the discussions? At the right time?
	Is there a clear process and timetable for more detailed action planning to be done inside the organization?
Implement-ation	Do we have the resources (skills, manpower, money, location, etc.) to do this?
	Are the financial projections which accompany this strategy realistic and viable?
	Is the deadline we are setting arbitrary – does our goal really need to be achieved by that date, or would a later date reduce the risk while maintaining the same level of benefit?
Oversight	What measures of both input and outcome are we establishing as we implement this particular strategy? Are these more than just a general set of operational and/or project measures?
	Which of our assumptions about the external market might change in future and how will we notice?
	What risks might materialize and require us to review or change our strategy?

About the future:
Talking about what's
over the horizon

Board meetings are often dominated by discussions about current activities, but looking outside and ahead is a key board responsibility. The temptation to focus on the present rather than the future is understandable: independent board members want to use their previous experience to add value to the here-and-now, while executive directors with direct responsibility for current operations have much that they want to discuss with the board.

But if the board doesn't look ahead, who will?

These future-focused conversations are a key part of the strategy process, but they are complex and it is easy to rush through them. That's why this book emphasizes conversations about horizon-scanning specifically – because the board needs to wrestle with ideas and insights about an unknown future as part of its strategy role.

Here is a set of ideas to make the conversation more effective, to use along with those in *Conversation 6*, because both these conversations are vital in developing effective strategy.

Talking about the future

Conversations about the future differ from the focused, overseeing conversations, which characterize a normal board meeting, and even from deliberations about strategy. The Institute of Risk Management calls them *'an alerting and creative activity'*.[29] Ideally, these should be imaginative, speculative conversations, probably with a wide range of different views about what might happen. But they are not easy conversations because they draw on *'the two least developed skills in the workplace: the ability to have uncomfortable conversations and the ability to ask "what if...?" questions'*.[30]

Future-oriented conversations can feel vague and uncomfortable because there are no right or wrong answers. The different sources of data vary in reliability and credibility and some views may be dismissed as being too unlikely to be worth discussing. Some board members may find long-held assumptions challenged and are therefore unwilling to engage in the discussion.

However, these conversations are vital, and board members need them to steer the organization through turbulent, uncertain and ambiguous contexts, in which new developments, events and crises will arise. The acronym TUNA (Turbulent, Uncertain, Novel and Ambiguous) is a variant on the VUCA description (Volatility, Uncertainty, Complexity and Ambiguity) and it reminds the board that their turbulent context will always bring something *novel* and unprecedented.

One interviewee commented that the best board conversation she ever participated in started with a 'magpie exercise': board members were asked to discuss six completely new developments about which they knew nothing and to assemble them into a view of a possible future – like mythical magpies collecting shiny objects to use in their nests. This exercise enabled the board to confront the shared information bias, where people tend to focus on the information that they all have, rather than new or unshared information. It also unleashed the creativity of the group.

Defining the task

Firstly, some framing: these conversations are about exploring multiple future possibilities. They are not about nailing down specific forecasts, but about noticing a wide range of indicators and speculating about their impact.

The board's role here is not prediction, but preparation – and the conversation itself is part of preparing the organization for an essentially unknowable future. There's a degree of mental priming in the discussion, even if the specific situations that the board imagined do not come to pass.

The task is not about deciding between a set of strategy options, or generating a list of actions for the strategy team. Rather, the point of these discussions is to ensure that the board has a shared set of ideas about what the context *might* be like in the medium and long term.

Finding and using data

Horizon-scanning is a sensing activity, fuelled by a range of data sources, of different kinds and of varying degrees of definiteness. The data sources are both external and internal; publications, industry events, websites, industry leaders, competitors, customers and suppliers have perspectives and insights to offer, as do staff at the operational edge of the business. The power of big data sets to improve operations or to reduce costs is already with us, but this future-focused conversation also needs to look at the new ideas or developments at the bleeding edge of innovation, which are weak signals of major changes ahead.

The board's conversation should, in particular, explore combinations of factors, which taken together may have more impact than they do singly – for example, economic downturn combined with a health crisis, or new developments in artificial intelligence in conjunction with a shift in social attitudes.

'Black swans'

Organizations must also look up from the data and watch for the unexpected out-of-the-blue disruptive events. These are sometimes described as 'black swans' – situations that were widely regarded as absolutely impossible, but which have then occurred, to universal astonishment.[31] The metaphor comes from the widespread belief that there was no such thing as a black swan, which was disproved when they were found to be commonplace in Australia.

This is a subjective description: what might feel like a black swan event to one observer may be more predictable and less startling to another. For many organizations and most people, the global COVID-19 pandemic was such a sudden and unprecedented event, but not for epidemiologists. And that is why these wide-ranging conversations around the boardroom table are so important: to share perspectives and overcome particular blind-spots or biases. And this is not an idle discussion: such events can have catastrophic effects on organizations, as history shows.

Exogenous and endogenous factors

As the board looks ahead, the conversations should cover both exogenous and endogenous factors.

- **Exogenous factors** are defined as those having an external cause or origin, sometimes visible, but rarely controllable. Many will typically be recorded in organizational risk registers, but this conversation is a chance to rethink this analysis. They might be global or local, large or small scale – for example, a global financial crisis or an especially cold winter in one part of the world affecting customers in that area.
- **Endogenous factors** are those which have an internal cause or origin. Because they tend to be visible and slightly more controllable, organizations may be able to plan their response. Examples include scheduled systems implementation dates, the expiry of an office lease, or the retirement dates for key senior leaders. Some organizations develop a planning calendar for

the foreseeable future, for a few years ahead, setting out what is already scheduled and must be accommodated. This perspective helps the board to see when the organization may be particularly busy and therefore less able to take on a new development, or when additional resources may be required to keep the operation running.

Conversations with a range of stakeholders about the future can reveal changes that the board was not aware of – for example, a key supplier planning to relocate, bringing possible disruption to the supply chain. And, of course, different stakeholders see the context differently, so their perspective is always worth having.

Identifying these factors is useful, but it is the interplay between the two which is key: two companies experiencing the same market changes (exogenous factors) may generate different results, because of their contrasting internal structures and resources (endogenous factors).

'Grey elephants'

And, in conversation, board members shouldn't ignore the 'grey elephants' – those factors or events that everyone in the organization knows could be problematic but which are moving so slowly that the board feels it has plenty of time to address them, solve the problems or prepare for their impact. Slow-moving endogenous factors sometimes speed up, though, so it is dangerous to dismiss them as a problem that can safely be left for tomorrow.

Three planning horizons

Thinking about the future is not simply looking ahead to the end of the year, but looking beyond to what might lie just over the horizon. The idea of three different horizons (see Figure 7.1) helps the board to hone its horizon-scanning processes so that they allocate sufficient attention to the unknown and distant, as well as what is around the corner.

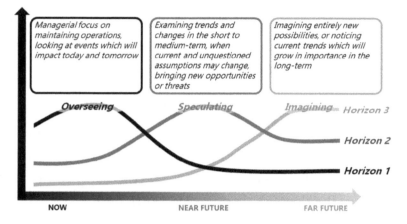

Figure 7.1   Three horizons for considering the future[32]

The three horizons model has various uses in developing strategy, with the phases defined in the following way.

- **Horizon 1 – NOW:** *Overseeing* current operations, looking at events which will impact today and tomorrow.
- **Horizon 2 – NEAR FUTURE:** *Speculating* about trends and changes in the short to medium term, when current and unquestioned assumptions may change, bringing new opportunities or threats.
- **Horizon 3 – FAR FUTURE:** *Imagining* entirely new possibilities, or noticing current trends which will grow in importance in the long term.

Horizon 1 is often the focus of the board's conversation, while Horizon 2 will often be the focus of specific strategy discussions. But the board needs to look at all three horizons and at the implications of each for the others. The model illustrates the overlaps: factors which will affect Horizon 2 may already be visible now – 'pockets of the future found in the present' – and those driving Horizon 3 may be just around the corner.

Scenario thinking

Since the future is essentially unknown, many organizations in turbulent contexts focus less on formal planning and more on developing the organizational flexibility to respond to whatever happens. One technique they use is to develop a range of possible scenarios about what might happen in future, to help them to see what the organization might have to do in response. The scenario method is regarded as 'a practical tool for collective strategic thinking' in an organization.[33]

This is not a tool for preparing for a *planned* future, but rather '*a disciplined method for imaging possible futures in which organizational decisions may be played out*'.[34]

The idea is to develop a set of narratives, or scenarios, about what might happen over a specific time period, covering a wide range of factors – social, economic, political, technological and environmental, for example. The board can then explore what effect a particular imagined future might have on the organization and how new opportunities and threats might appear as a result. The conversation also looks at the forces that might cause each scenario to be realized – for example, major social changes or an environmental crisis.

This scenario approach is useful for boards both at the start of the strategy thinking and as the work comes to a conclusion. At the outset, the opening analysis of opportunities and threats facing the organization may look different in the context of different possible future scenarios. Towards the end of the strategy review, those same scenarios also serve as a means of testing the strategy to see how it plays out in different possible futures. And articulating and testing the assumptions in the strategy to see how long they will remain accurate in different scenarios helps in developing robust plans.

Board roles and routines

Many of the techniques and approaches described above are obviously useful for boards as part of the specific strategy workshops and away-days, but the board needs to have regular conversations about what is happening outside the organization. Horizon-scanning is not a once-and-done activity.

The board meeting is the place where both internal and the external factors should be brought together in the service of good decisions and timely actions. Some simple routines will help the board to balance the discussion appropriately, so that conversations about the future and the external are not squeezed out by a focus on the present and the internal. For example, allocating individual board members to monitor a particular external trend, such as regulatory change or developments with a key technology, helps with this. The meeting agenda should allow time for updates on such developments, which may or may not be significant – the collective conversation will help to establish whether they are or are not. Alternatively, starting the board discussion with a round-table conversation prompted by the question *'What have you noticed happening in our sector this month?'* signals the need for board members to stay attentive to their context and to bring insights into the board's conversations.

The different styles and approaches of board members helps these conversations, too: for example, natural pessimists are often skilled at generating scenarios, while their more optimistic colleagues balance out the debate. This is one more example of the importance of a diverse board, with a range of different approaches to this vital strategic conversation.

Case study: Imagining a possible future

In order to illustrate the power of recognizing a potential Horizon 3 change and capitalizing on it, this case comes from the early

2000s, to show the way in which imagining a distant possible future shaped the organization's strategy, and what happened as a result.

In 2000, an academic book distributor noticed that academic journals were increasingly available as downloadable electronic resources. As they looked ahead, they wondered about what would happen to their book distribution business if books also became digital. Recognizing this potential Horizon 3 problem, they started to invest in building a platform for digitizing physical books and making them available electronically to academic libraries.

By 2006 they had built one of the few viable eBook platforms, which was then acquired by a major corporation. Their ability to look far enough ahead had given them time to turn a potential threat looming over the horizon into a competitive advantage.

Summary

- Boards must spend time thinking and talking about the future, not simply at the annual strategy workshop.
- These conversations are about exploring multiple future possibilities, rather than making specific predictions, and they are never easy.
- Horizon-scanning is a sensing activity, drawing on a wide range of data sources.
- Board discussion should cover both *endogenous factors* (internal events that are largely known) as well as *exogenous factors* (insights about the external context).
- Conversations about 'black swans' and 'grey elephants' help the board to develop a shared sense of what might lie ahead.
- Looking ahead can cover three horizons:
  - *Horizon 1* – the near future;
  - *Horizon 2* – the short to medium term;
  - *Horizon 3* – the distant future.

- The scenario method is a way of structuring the collective thinking to generate rigorous conversations.
- Board roles and routines can make these conversations more likely to happen.

Checklist: Topics for conversations about the future

Horizon	Endogenous	Exogenous
1	What are the key events which we have planned in the next 12 to 24 months and when are they scheduled to happen?	What might happen in our context or market in the short term – those things that might affect us this year (e.g., competitor activity, regulatory change, technological development, etc.)?
2	What are the 'grey elephants' – those events or factors that we know will affect us in future but which we may have been ignoring because they appear to be moving so slowly?	What have we noticed happening in our context recently that this organization might need to respond to in the near future?
		What kind of disruptive event might occur in the near future – a 'black swan' event?
3		What new trend or development might transform our market or context? What might change politically or in the economy, in society and social attitudes, through technology or new legal requirements or in the environment that would radically alter our market or geography? [The PESTEL framework]

Horizon	Endogenous	Exogenous
3		Which of these scenarios might be positive for this organization and why? Which would be negative and why?
Assurance questions for the board	Are we as a board spending the right amount of time looking up, ahead and out – as opposed to inside, down and at the present operation?	What sources of information and insight about the external world do we have? Are they reliable, and sufficient?
	Are management in this organization attentive to future changes – and how do we know?	

About holding to account: Creating a culture of accountability

G iven the board's responsibilities for managerial oversight, some conversations in board meetings must be about holding people to account, as a fundamental part of board governance. But the board is also responsible for creating an open and honest culture of accountability, and it can feel as if doing one gets in the way of the other.

Understanding the difficulties that may arise in holding to account and how to overcome them is vital. This will help to foster the open dialogue that is vital in creating accountability in the boardroom.

The difficulties

Holding to account is traditionally viewed as a control activity, with regular routines of 'question-and-answer'. This is Mode A working, as described in *Conversation 2: About the board*. But there are four particular issues that make these board conversations difficult.

Issue 1

The scrutiny routine can reinforce a sense of a two-tier board, with some members of the board (independent members) checking the work of others (executive members). Even the definition of scrutiny – 'critical observation or examination' – can be misinterpreted in practice. 'Critical' is often taken to mean the expression of adverse comments, whereas it is actually a reference to analysis of *both* the merits and faults. In other words, 'critical' should be a description of the quality of the analysis, not of the tone in which questions are asked.

Issue 2

There is always an information asymmetry problem: independent board members need to hold executives to account without second-guessing every decision they make, but those whose decisions and actions are being scrutinized by the board have more information than those required to exercise scrutiny.

Issue 3

There are boundary issues – board members need to recognize executive responsibilities for running the business, while the board's role is to oversee it. This requires board members to explore and to ask questions, rather than to make statements about how they think things should be done or to issue detailed instructions. And for independent board members with extensive operational experience and a strong desire to add value, keeping to the right side of the line is not always easy.

Issue 4

This 'holding to account' conversation can feel as if it gets in the way of the other conversations the board needs to have: those that build relationships or the generative conversations to formulate strategy. But boards need to be able to have a forensic discussion about an idea, proposal, plan or decision, without killing it, or irreparably damaging the working relationships that are so key to transparency. They need to be able to 'put their finger lightly on the bruise' rather than poking it so hard that the executive retreats from the pain.

The wrong kinds of conversation bring real risks. Board members anxious about their duties may demand more explanations and yet more information and become terrier-like in search of answers and assurance. And, if they don't fully understand the operational realities, their challenge may be seen as unfair and corrosive. Overdoing scrutiny can weary executives; they start to feel that their job is mostly about feeding the board with data, some not very informative. And if the board regularly gets lost in a welter of detail, executives may feel that board meetings add no value, but simply consume time.

Creating a culture of accountability

The right kinds of conversations, though, create a culture of accountability: executives are clear about their responsibilities and motivated to achieve them, and the board's conversations build a commitment to the actions that have been agreed.

As Roberts et al. describe: '*Such accountability is a practice achieved through a wide variety of behaviours – challenging, questioning, probing, discussing, testing, informing, debating, exploring, encouraging – that are at the very heart of how non-executives seek to be effective*.'[35]

Independent board members can create a virtuous circle, in which their well-informed interest generates good questions and productive debate, which executives find valuable. For that reason, it becomes increasingly worthwhile to bring issues to the board for discussion, and thus a culture of openness develops. This, in turn, increases mutual trust, which sets the tone for constructive conversations that hold to account.

Three key ingredients

Three aspects of the board's work are central in generating this virtuous circle:

1. appropriate structures and processes for 'holding to account' conversations;
2. basing the conversations on relevant information;
3. framing the style, scope and tone of such discussions.

Processes and structures for holding to account

Boardroom conversations can't do all the work of holding to account without appropriate processes and structures – for delegation, for control and for reporting as part of the board's 'watchful and responsible care'. If these processes are working, holding to account becomes part and parcel of the way things are done in the organization.

For example, in the course of the year, the board might have a series of in-depth discussions about key topics. The annual schedule could be designed to allow reviews of each of the main areas of work over the year. And committee scrutiny in a smaller meeting allows for more searching conversations, which can then be reported to the board for assurance purposes.

Information for accountability

Information asymmetry is a fact of boardroom life. Some board members try to solve this problem by relying too much on their own executive experience from a different organization, at a different time. Monologues about what they did when they were an executive or a CEO rarely land well and irritate executives, because the current organization and its context is always different.

The solution lies in using the right kind of board data pack to fuel board scrutiny.

Board data packs

The board will want to agree what the reporting pack looks like, and, particularly, to specify the key indicators to be reported, based on the organization's strategy. Ideally, board members should have a sense of the rate of progress they are expecting in these metrics. Regular, standardized reporting will allow them to track trends – changing the report formats too often may obscure those insights. One characteristic is particularly important: every board paper should set out clearly what is needed – either approval for a decision, or a discussion to review progress, or simply to note the information.

The right amount of data

The information asymmetry problem can't be solved by asking hundreds of detailed questions, hoping that when you know enough about the matter in hand you will know as much as your executive colleagues do, and therefore you will be able to scrutinize it fully. In fact, boards might usefully ask themselves whether they are getting too much data – obscuring the focus on things that matter – rather than too little.

The assumption that more data leads to better decisions is only true up to a point. The curve is actually U-shaped: more leads to better decisions only up to the point of information overload. When 'the wood can't be seen for the trees', board members spend time digesting data rather than working out what is really going on.

And sometimes, the data the board asks for may be unobtainable, or take time to prepare. Constant requests for more data, or different cuts of the existing data, consume staff time, so board members need to be sure that the benefit is worth the effort.

Data at the right level of detail

If the papers are too detailed, the board's conversation will also be too detailed. In a continued effort to make a contribution, board members may raise questions that are superficial or trivial. So, priming the conversation with data at the appropriate level is vital. The test is: does this paper help us to see whether we are on course in implementing our strategy?

This is the reason that many boards use a template for their papers, to ensure that each paper covers the connection to the overarching purpose and strategy, any impact on staff, customers and other stakeholders, or changes to the risk profile.

The right kinds of data

Examine what the board pack contains: is it mostly facts or interpretations of the facts? Ideally, a healthy balance of both is needed, and the board needs to be clear which is which. Patrick Dunne, in his book on boards, offers useful micro-technique for reading board papers and literally marking them up with either F for fact, or I for interpretation.[36] And some facts are more useful than others: for example, board papers which recount the number of awards won by the organization may distract the board from more significant information.

At the right stage of development

Boards need to know whether the paper that has come to the board is finished and ready for approval, or whether it is still work in progress, which they can contribute to and influence before the work is finished. Board members often ask that they be given sight of work in progress so that they can exercise direction and shape the work, but then sometimes complain about the incompleteness of the paper.

Options

To be sure that preparatory work has been comprehensive, many boards insist that there are options in board proposals, as well as a recommendation with reasons. There is always more than one choice, even if it's simply to do nothing.

Board members might also consider whether the options are presented in order to steer them in one particular direction. It's worth knowing which option the executive team prefers, but the board may wish to think about whether there has been sufficient consideration of alternatives and whether the reasons for the recommendation are good enough.

Context

Are you and the board looking at the data in the right context? Executives may be held to account for implementing the strategy that the board has approved, but the board is accountable for the strategy's suitability in its current market. Has the context changed so much that the strategy is no longer viable? The board conversation is the place where these two perspectives – internal and external – come together, to be sure that the organization is still doing the right things.

Data from the team working on the issue

Do members of staff who have actually been working on the topic come in to the meeting, either to present or to listen to the board's discussion? Direct interaction with the board helps the discussion and may well help the team, too. But these conversations require a degree of care: more junior members of staff may not be expecting to be held to account in a rigorous debate about the topic they have been working on.

Conversational framing

By holding someone to account, the board acknowledges that it is that person's proper responsibility – they must respect the boundaries between the executive role and the board's role. It's a key part of the chair's responsibility to watch for this, and there is more about this in *Conversation 3: About chairing*. The obvious truth that board members are *directing, not doing*, is nowhere more important than in these conversations. This framing helps to shift the conversation from control to respectful oversight, and avoids the temptation of micro-management.

Scope

Holding to account covers present operations and future plans, insights and ideas, not just today's numbers. It is not simply focused on the areas of particular interest to individual board members. Good conversations allow space to connect activities back to the organization's purpose, to look for alignment between what the organization says it is about and what it actually does. Misalignment – investing in areas that don't seem to be central to the organization's purpose, or outside its current strategy – is something to watch for. It may be an investment in strategic diversification, but it can also be the cause of excessive cost, value destruction, confusion, loss of productivity and reduced staff morale.[37]

Style

It goes without saying that the manner of the conversation should be courteous, respectful and collaborative. For example, a question that comes from a genuine and informed interest generates a different kind of discussion from one that looks as if it is aiming to catch someone out. The conversations should allow executives to 'tell it like it is', with the right topics being discussed, rather than carefully omitted from the agenda because the executives feel it's too difficult and painful to get the board involved. People in organizations watch closely how boards exercise oversight, particularly when there is a problem, and the interactions round the boardroom table have a disproportionate effect on company culture, for good or ill.

Exploring and explaining

These conversations ideally allow time to explore the issue and the actions being taken. Try this test: if someone can't explain their plan or decision so that an intelligent 10-year-old could understand it, then they don't understand it well enough themselves, and the board won't either. In the film *Margin Call*, at a crisis board meeting, the chair, played by Jeremy Irons, instructs one of the executives to explain what's happening clearly: '*Speak as you might to a young child or a golden retriever*'. If it's still not clear enough for a board discussion, more work is needed outside the board meeting.

Questioning

Good questions clarify, probe assumptions and rationale; they illuminate, and possibly change perspectives, as long as there is attentive listening to the answers. Technique 5 in the *Introduction* to this book explores the use of powerful questions as part of the board member's conversational repertoire. There is also huge power in the second, follow-up question. For example, '*What does this mean for our customers?*' or '*How would we actually realize this cost-saving?*' Some of these questions might appear naive to the expert executive, but they can uncover important implications, or hidden assumptions.

The ideal boardroom culture allows an executive who doesn't immediately know the answer to the question to say so. Much damage is done in organizations by someone nervously making up a wrong answer to a question instead of being able to say: '*That's a good question and I will get back to you with a good answer*'.

The checklist at the end of this conversation sets out a series of generic questions for board members, both to ask and to reflect on. But questioning works both ways: it is a good indicator of a positive culture of accountability if executives ask questions of independent board members, seeking advice.

Case study: Inappropriate scrutiny

In one organization, the board's focus on the process of holding to account became a regular, almost ritual, interrogation of the CEO and executive colleagues, about every topic, large or small. And the more questions asked by independent board members, the more detail was supplied in the papers.

On the face of it, the board was doing its job: scrutinizing progress, asking questions about key activities, and challenging assumptions. But the detailed, corrosive scrutiny damaged inter-actions with the executive, and the culture of the organization as a whole. Any complex issue would incur a raft of aggressive ques-tions, sometimes focused on trivial or incidental aspects. Staff members attending a board meeting to present on a particular topic would be shocked into silence by the tone of the questioning. And they would, understandably, comment on this to colleagues when returning to their desks.

As a consequence, over time, the board agenda became less and less significant: controversial topics were avoided, or taken in committee, and board papers increasingly focused on PR activities and awards, rather than key strategic matters.

This situation required a set of changes: a new chair was appointed, the board undertook some training and team building, and, slowly, working relationships were repaired.

Summary

- Holding to account is a fundamental part of governance, but organizations also need a culture of accountability.
- There are some real difficulties:
    - the information asymmetry problem;
    - the boundaries of the roles, so that independent board members are directing and not doing;
    - the 'holding to account' conversation involves questioning, rather than interrogation, focusing on the actions rather than the person, and balancing challenge and support appropriately.

- The wrong kinds of conversation, with excessive, uninformed scrutiny, do not get to the real issues, descend into unimportant detail and damage working relationships.
- The right kinds of conversation create a virtuous circle and generate a culture of accountability.
- Three particular aspects of these conversations are key:
  - appropriate structures and processes;
  - drawing on relevant information;
  - framing the style, scope and tone of such discussions.
- The boardroom is a place where external and internal insights are brought together to be sure that the organization is doing the right things, and accountable for 'doing them right'.

Checklist: Questions for conversations and board reflection

Questions for conversations
When reviewing proposals for decision
• How did we reach this conclusion?
• What other options did we consider? Were there any options we excluded from the start? Why make this recommendation?
• What assumptions are we making about the organization and our context as we recommend this option? Do they make sense?
• Would you do this if it were your own money?
• What are the risks – and are we sure they aren't also opportunities for us?
• Can we actually do this? Who specifically will implement this and do they have the right resources?
• Is this in line with our purpose as an organization?
• How will this affect our customers/staff/stakeholders/shareholders/funders – what is the impact on each group?
• What could go wrong for us? What if this fails – do we have a back-up plan and what is it?

When reviewing progress
• To what extent is this investment, or this set of operational results moving the organization forward towards its desired outcome - or not?
• What did we plan to do in this reporting period and have we been able to do it?
• What has held us up? What has helped us?
• Do we need to re-plan, and what effect will that have on resources and outcomes?
• Do we have contingency and have we used it?
• Do we have a back-up plan?
• What did we learn from this – and what would we do differently in future?
On overall performance
• What were the measures of success we set out and how are we performing against them?
• What do we need to do to improve our performance?
• Are these results what we predicted would happen and if not, why not?

Questions for board reflection
Are we holding to account effectively – with courteous, constructive conversations that uncover what is really happening and why?
Does our board data pack serve the board well?
Do we have the right information regularly presented to us so that we can see what's going on?
Is it at the right level of detail – appropriately strategic?
Does it help us to see how the implementation of our strategy is going?

About people and reward: Development, succession and remuneration

Conversations about the people in the organization must be high on the agenda for boards and conversations *with* staff are a key part of the board's leadership role. Staff are key stakeholders, and people with the right skills are not easy to find and keep. The pandemic has created new working patterns and considerations of equality, diversity and inclusion are more important than ever, while the global cost-of-living crisis in 2023 encouraged boards to be more involved with employee issues.

The board is responsible for ensuring that the organization has the resources necessary to implement the strategy and enact its purpose – and this means people. Conversations about people issues span the strategic to the specific, and they matter hugely. Some will take place with the whole board, because the board will want assurance about the remuneration approach for the whole organization, for example. Others are committee discussions, such as specific decisions on senior pay or succession planning for key posts. And some conversations will be about the board's own succession plans, to ensure that it has the necessary skills for good governance.

The board's attention to people issues is particularly important in two areas: first, the ethical and fair approach taken to employees and employment; and, second, the alignment between the organization's purpose and its policies for people. Every decision made about people issues at the board or in the HR function affects the organization's ability to implement its plans and live out its purpose. For example, the shape of the employment package or the investment in development for staff affect the organization's ability to recruit, retain and motivate.

In some contexts, though, the board may have less control over these matters, as for example in public boards where pay arrangements are set by central civil service functions. But whether they have control or not, the board must still understand and oversee the way people are recruited, how they are paid, and how their performance is managed and assessed.

Fuelling the conversations with data

This requires data to come to the board regularly: staff turnover or sickness and absence figures will usually come to the board at a summary level, but reports on staff well-being and morale should also be discussed, using results from staff surveys. But while executives take a close operational view, the board should look at these indicators in the light of their purpose, strategic goals and values. These data tell the board whether the organization is translating its purpose and mission into a culture that has meaning for people and which inspires them.

Sometimes, more detail can be useful; some boards, or their committees, will ask to see summaries of exit interviews, to understand more about why employees are leaving, or look at staff survey data at the department level, comparing them with performance. But such conversations should be occasional, because they may tempt the board to trespass into operational matters and distract them from the strategic view. Sometimes, external data from social media sites such as The Student Room and Glassdoor can also be insightful – see resources in the *Appendix*.

Conversations about equality, diversity and inclusion

The board has a key role in overseeing the matters of equality, diversity and inclusion, both in terms of policies and practices. If the board itself is diverse, that sends a powerful signal to the organization and the outside world. It also helps if at least one independent board member has experience of working in this area because this is increasingly a more specialized and professional activity.

These conversations are not just about recruitment and pay, but about every aspect of the organization: product and service delivery, as well as performance management and promotion. Discussions will be about obstacles in the systems, as well as development needs for individuals, and they need to be based on good demographic data.

The board will want to talk with the HR team about a planned approach, covering all aspects of these important matters. Some organizations set themselves specific targets and monitor progress, while others focus on a range of initiatives, recognizing the complexity of the situations different people face. Increasingly, the board will be expected to report on progress on a basket of indicators, including, for example, the gender pay gap.

External data and insight fuel these conversations, too: there is much to learn from other organizations, in different sectors, and the board will want to be familiar with national initiatives, such as the 30% Club, as well as major reviews such as the Parker Review.[38]

Visible leadership in this area helps hugely and the key success factor here is to keep this topic on the agenda and to have regular conversations about it.

Organization and job design

Post-pandemic, many organizations see a wider range of working patterns, blending in-office with remote working. This has created new pressures, which the board must be aware of: for example, not everyone can work remotely and this may create a division in the organization. Promotion and appraisal processes will need to operate differently in an age of hybrid working, and team structure and work allocation may need to change depending on the working locations for staff. The board needs to be sure that these matters are being considered, because they are so important to the organization's ability to deliver, as well as to employee morale.

Internal transformation projects often have significant implications for staff, so it is always worth asking about the impact on people and how it is being managed. To take a specific example, the creation of a new business school at a university required a new building, but the strategic intention was also to create new ways of working – closer team structures and on-site collaboration with multiple external partners. The board did not simply focus on the progress of the building work, but also on how the building would be designed with new ways of working in mind.

Recruiting senior leaders

One of the most important activities for board members is their involvement in the recruitment process for senior leaders, particularly the CEO, and sometimes for a new chair of the board. This work is often performed by a Nominations Committee (NomCo) as a sub-committee of the board. And here too, as in the board overall, the remit has become wider and the approach more professional.

It used to be that the NomCo was regarded as the 'Cinderella' of board committees, but not so now. The committee will have accountability for the appointment process for senior roles, and for succession planning, including assessing the strength of the talent in the levels below the board. Terms of reference for these committees vary by sector, but the UK Financial Reporting Council's definition of the role illustrates the breadth of its work: the committee oversees a *continuous and proactive process of planning and assessment, taking into account the company's strategic priorities and the main trends and factors affecting the long-term successes and future viability of the company*.[39]

Conversations in this committee need to be about the strategic as well as the tactical. At the strategic level, the committee must ensure that its work is driven by, and contributes to, the organization's overall strategy as well as the people strategies for talent management and diversity. At the tactical level, conversations will cover the choreography between the departures and arrivals of the key boardroom players – specifically the chair, the CEO, the finance director and, in some contexts, the senior independent director. These conversations can be difficult: it is not always easy to establish the plans of key leaders, and it can be hard to challenge those plans if they are not in the best interests of the organization. But missing the opportunity for those discussions risks losing good people. As one senior leader commented, sadly: *'I was expecting someone to begin a discussion with me about a new role, but the job I really wanted has just been filled. Nobody thought to talk to me about it and I feel as though I have no option now but to leave'.*

Appointing a CEO or the most senior leader

The board has oversight of the recruitment approach for this key role, and – as in any recruitment process – some choices to make. For example, will the process be handled in-house, or be led by a search consultancy? How wide will the search for the right person be and what assessment and interview processes will be used? How much should the appointed person be paid, and how will their remuneration be structured?

The choices will be influenced by previous experience and what is normally done in this sector. For example, public sector and charitable organizations will usually be expected to advertise vacancies externally, candidates may well be aware of who else is applying, and there is an expectation that people in the organization will be involved in the process. But in the private sector, the process may be less formal, and the role may not be advertised at all, even internally.

Most important, though, is the definition of the role. Here, the board should be explicit about its expectations, both in their boardroom discussions and with the candidate. For example, will the candidate be expected to devote all their time to this role, or would they be able to continue with any existing independent board roles elsewhere?

Candidates will want to understand whether the role is do-able given the culture of the organization and the likely working relationship with the board. There are several organizations where a new senior leader was brought in with a mission to make change, but later removed by the board when that change was subsequently resisted by employees – and by board members themselves.

Board resilience and succession

The conversation about board succession planning is equally crucial, and spans discussions about executive and independent board members with particular skills.

The board should have a register of current skills round the boardroom table, as well as those they expect to need, given the organization's plans for the future. There should also be a schedule of the dates for terms of office, so that board membership can be synchronized to avoid mass departures at any one point. The board needs continuity as well as refreshed membership and this balance needs to be managed. Most boards find it helpful to get into the habit of having these discussions and to be explicit from the outset about terms of office.

Ideally, NomCo members should know something about the potential candidates for executive board roles at the levels below the board. This might involve reviewing data about performance and potential, as well ensuring that potential candidates get the development opportunities they need. External assessment and benchmarking might be a route to gain insight into potential candidates, but it helps if independent board members can find an opportunity to meet them and see them in action.

Remuneration structures

How does your organization reward staff, and how does that compare to competitors, or others in the same sector? Increasingly, organizations build a range of benefits into the remuneration for staff, including, for example, health plans, pension options or childcare support, so comparison is not always easy. However, board members should have a view of the relative rates of remuneration and reward because they want to be able to employ people with the skills they need and pay them appropriately and fairly.

Remuneration Committee

Some independent board members will serve on the Remuneration Committee (RemCo) as a sub-committee of the board. Their role is to ensure that the remuneration policy and practices are aligned with the organization's purpose and values, and will therefore help the organization to deliver its strategic plans. To do this, independent board members need to understand how the structure works and ensure that it is used fairly.

The committee will typically have specific responsibility for the shape and quantum of the remuneration of the senior team, including base pay, bonuses, benefits and pensions. This is an important area of oversight and can be surprisingly onerous. The complexity of some schemes can be hard to navigate, and appropriate levels of reward difficult to assess, as the case study at the end of this conversation illustrates. This is particularly true as measures of performance move beyond the short-term and the financial: for example, some bonus schemes now include a set of factors about progress on environmental, social and governance (ESG) matters, intended to measure the organization's impact on society, the environment, and how transparent and accountable it is.

Committee discussions also require transparency. The committee must be aware of actual or potential conflicts of interest in every meeting – and individuals whose remuneration arrangements are under discussion should not be in the room, or involved in those discussions in any way.

Remuneration is a complex matter and very often RemCo will commission external consultants to advise them, although responsibility for the decisions remains with the committee and, ultimately, the board.

Remuneration arrangements may also be scrutinized externally by regulators, specific stakeholders, the press or indeed the public. Where there are investors, they may look to influence these matters, either through discussions with the chair of RemCo or through voting at the annual general meeting (AGM). Annual reports reveal how rewards to senior leaders are matched by performance, and how senior remuneration compares with average employee pay. The committee may also have to report on what kind of workforce engagement has taken place to explain how executive remuneration aligns with wider company pay policy.

Case study: Unintended consequences of bonus scheme design

In 2017, the former CEO of the house-builder Persimmon received a payment of over £100 million as part of a bonus scheme. The scheme was set up to recognize performance, but the results were largely driven by a UK government 'Right to Buy Scheme' funded by UK tax payers. Public and media reaction to the bonus payment was vociferous, labelling it 'obscene' and 'corporate looting'.

As a consequence, the chair of the organization resigned, stating that he regretted that the scheme had not been capped, and he was leaving 'in recognition of this omission'.[40]

Summary

- Staff are key stakeholders and conversations about people must be high on the board agenda.
- The board is responsible for ensuring that the organization has the skills and resources it needs, and that they are treated ethically and paid fairly, in line with the strategy.
- These conversations are built on the board's examination of the data, including staff well-being and motivation, and the board must consider policies and practices in the light of the emphasis on equality, diversity and inclusion.
- Oversight of remuneration structures may be delegated to the RemCo, which will also make recommendations on specific senior pay decisions for board approval.
- The NomCo may oversee succession planning for the organization and the board, as well as recruitment of senior leaders, particularly the CEO.

Checklist: Questions for reflection

People strategy and equality, diversity and inclusion
Do we have a people strategy, and does it support the organization's strategy? How do we know?
How diverse is the organization? What actions are being taken on equality, diversity and inclusion and are they part of a planned approach?
How is the board demonstrating their commitment to these matters?
Has the board set targets for the organization and is good progress being made?
Remuneration for the senior team
Is your organization's remuneration strategy coherent and aligned to the business strategy?
How does the remuneration of the CEO compare to the rest of the senior team? To the rest of the organization?
Are financial rewards of overall performance shared, and, if so, how?

| How strong is the link between remuneration and performance – in the short and the long term? |
| If ESG measures are included in the remuneration scheme, are they clear and strategically significant? Are the thresholds for payment suitably demanding? |
| **Succession** |
| Do we have a clear schedule as to when senior people at the organization will be moving on? |
| What is the basis on which their contracts will end (e.g., fixed-term contracts)? |
| What are the key roles for which we should have a succession plan? Does the board have assurance that there is a realistic plan? |
| How well do we as board members know people in the top two levels of the organization? |

About effectiveness: Talking about board performance

The practice of reviewing the board's effectiveness is both useful and required – and if your board is not undertaking some form of purposeful reflection on what they do and how they do it, you will definitely want to ask why not. The board that is responsible for overseeing the performance of the organization should be reviewing its own performance. Even good boards occasionally falter and the key to improvement is to talk about it.

The central idea here is that combining formal reviews with regular informal conversations about effectiveness makes this part of the way the board works, rather than a topic which is only addressed once a year. Review conversations work better if they are part of a collective reflective habit. But in every case, the board members themselves should choose the way their own reviews work, both formally and informally. There are a range of options for boards set out here, along with some guidance for the conversations and for the data that fuels them.

Effectiveness reviews: An overview

In many sectors, the regulatory guidance recommends some form of review each year, and may require that an external review takes place every three or five years. This will be a scheduled, collective activity, focusing both on behaviours and outcomes.[41]

Annual effectiveness reviews are the opportunity for the board to reflect on and assess the full range of its collective activities: internal managerial oversight, external stakeholder engagement, as well as its leadership of the organization. Reviews should look at outcomes: one interviewee commented that, in his sector, the board's performance was often evaluated simply by the increase in share price during their term of office, or the sale value at the end of it. However, the review process should look at both outcomes and behaviours together, because there are examples of boards with glowing effectiveness reviews and poor results.

Some boards avoid such reviews – or do them rather perfunctorily – because of the concern that the process will turn out to be a series of individual appraisal meetings. Although this is not a traditional performance management conversation, some boards consciously create the opportunity for members to reflect on, and talk about, their own contributions as part of the review process, as discussed in the next section.

Reasons to do a review

Aside from the regulatory requirements, a review of collective effectiveness is valuable in various ways.

Review conversations often identify ways to improve efficiency, through stronger administrative support, or a different meeting schedule, for example. They allow the board to plan ahead: for example, a board might agree to set each member an area of focus for the year ahead, or define particular milestones for the board as a whole to achieve.

A well-designed review process can also surface any issues that might get in the way of effective working. For example, board members may be concerned about a topic that never appears on meeting agendas, or feel that they do not have sufficient time to spend on strategic matters. Conversations are the key to this, allowing board members to connect, and to reflect. They are an opportunity to 'click the board's reset button'.

One by-product of such conversations is that members may get to know each other better and this pays off in tangible ways. If board members know each other well enough to recognize their individual strengths, and perhaps their blind spots, the sum of the parts really can be increased. Boardroom conversations become more efficient because people understand why a colleague may express particular views, with less need to explain.

The scope of the review: Content and conduct

Most guidance suggests that reviews of effectiveness should cover the underpinning structures and processes, as well as how the board behaves when they are together. The CEO of the UK Financial Reporting Council sums this up: 'the mechanical and tangible must be overlaid with the intangible'.[42] In other words, the scope covers both *content* – what the board does – and *conduct* – how it does it.

Content is about the areas of focus for the board and what is on the agenda for meetings. For example, is there sufficient attention to purpose, ethics and matters of stewardship? Does the board talk about real risks, rather than simply surveying the risk register? When they scrutinize present operations, do board members have the right kinds of data? Is the financial information they receive clear and understandable?

Conduct is about both process and behaviour – literally, how the board conducts its business. So, under this heading, the review conversation will cover basic process issues – for example, the timing of meetings and the dispatch of papers. But it will also look at more profound issues, such as how the board lives up to the organization's values. The board will want to talk about how they work together as an effective working group. They will want to consider the diversity and range of skills round the boardroom table, and whether all voices are heard.

Since the board's conduct is a function of the way individuals behave, too, some boards set up a peer review process, to provide mutual feedback.

There is a range of guidance about the scope of effectiveness reviews, from regulators, inspectors, trade or professional bodies and consultants. For example, in the UK, the National Audit Office offers a sample questionnaire[43] and the Financial Reporting Council's *Guidance on board effectiveness* (2018) contains sample questions suitable for use in many contexts. Some organizations will want their review to follow the scope of the inspection and regulatory regime in which they work.

Reviewing effectiveness: A board decision

Boards should have a conversation every so often about how and when they want to review their effectiveness, because there are choices to be made. The chair of the board or a particular committee will often initiate the process, given their responsibility for performance. Because this is a shared endeavour to make the board as effective as it can be, board members need to talk about how they want the process to work.

The approach they take will depend on a range of factors: for example, the relative experience of board members, or the current delivery pressures. The board might, for example, decide that, given their workload, they will run one formal review at the end of the financial year. Alternatively, a board might decide to add interim conversations every quarter, or to hold a review discussion both at the start and the end of the working year.

If the review process is designed carefully to suit the context, agreed with the board as a whole, and has a clear timetable with ground rules about appropriate confidentiality, it becomes a part of the way the board works, rather than an uncomfortable, artificial event.

Choices for the board

There is a set of choices about review conversations: style, timing and process, data sources and whether the board also wants to include reviews of individual contributions.

Style

Review conversations vary in style: they can be formal, scheduled exercises in line with regulatory requirements, or supplemented with informal, end-of-meeting conversations. They may be designed and led by the chair, or delivered by an external facilitator. Conversations may be based on immediate reactions from board members, or draw on survey data with a range of views from staff and stakeholders. And they may be collective conversations, or might also involve an individual self-assessment process, giving board members a chance to reflect on their own contributions, either in one-to-one conversations with the chair, or with an external facilitator.

Timing

In addition to the annual review of effectiveness, whether internal or external, some boards schedule a regular item at the end of each board meeting to review, briefly and informally, whether the meeting itself was effective. This has the advantage of building into the board's work a regular conversation about effectiveness, but boards may find that the pressure of time at the end of the agenda makes it too brief to be really useful. Alternatively, effectiveness could also be on the agenda for the chair's regular meetings with independent members. Or a board might also choose to do a short, informal review immediately after a major event, such as an acquisition, seizing the moment to reflect on what happened and what they might do differently as a board in future.

Process

Figure 10.1 illustrates the range of choices in designing a review process.

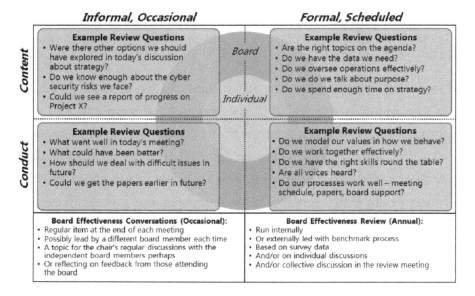

Figure 10.1   Conversations about board effectiveness

The figure illustrates the suggestion that boards should review their own effectiveness in various ways over the course of a one-, two- or three-year cycle: formally and informally, regularly and annually, and focused on content and conduct.

Exactly how they do this depends on the board's context. For example, a new board might choose to run a simple, entirely internal process, drawing on the views of board members only, and focused on their collective working. A long-standing board, by contrast, might find a formal review more useful, drawing on views of those who work with the board, not just board members. For a board where members don't know each other well, or don't interact constructively, it might help to have a formal review, led by an external facilitator, looking both at their own evaluation of individual contribution and collective effectiveness, benchmarked against other boards. During the global pandemic, many boards deliberately chose informal, light-touch reviews as they grappled with a range of completely new issues.

The checklist at the end of this conversation identifies the range of choices, to make it easier for the board as a whole to have a conversation about how exactly they want their review process to work.

Data sources

Good conversations need something to work from and, once again, there are some choices. Informal reviews could be based simply on a conversation at the end of a meeting about what worked well and what worked less well. Alternatively, a more formal review conversation might draw on both qualitative and quantitative data from a survey, or from individual interviews inside and outside the board, carried out by an external reviewer.

Survey data

If the board undertakes a formal survey to gather data, there are plenty of example survey questions and the *Appendix* suggests some useful websites. But there are some traps to avoid in designing survey questions. For example:

- Qualitative feedback, appropriately anonymous, is always useful, but needs to be taken in the round. In other words, if there is only one comment about something, the board should discuss it before making changes.
- Questions that ask for comment should also ask for specific actionable suggestions: for example, not just *'Are our board agendas appropriate?'* but *'What would you like to see added to the board meeting agenda over the next year?'*

- Where the question is quantitative, requiring a response from a scale, to avoid responses which are simply down the middle of the range (e.g., a score of 3 out of 5 on every question), you may want to use an even number (e.g., a scale from 1 to 4).

Staff feedback

The data set might also include feedback from staff in the organization, those who attend the board or who support its work. This can provide real insights, but it needs to be handled carefully. Simply accepting the survey results and making no response might reduce staff willingness to contribute in future. On the other hand, some staff suggestions may not be within the board's control, because they are part of some wider problem. For example, during the pandemic lockdowns, an assessment from staff that the board members were providing less visible leadership than usual was understandable since everyone was working remotely.

Benchmarking

External benchmarking data, offering comparisons with other similar boards in the same or related sectors, are likely to focus on specific metrics, such as frequency of board meetings, size of board or attendance levels. It may therefore need to be supplemented with one or more of the data sources already noted.

Collective conversations

At the heart of a good review process is the round-the-table discussion that gives all board members the chance to express their views, ideas and concerns in a safe and productive conversational space.

This conversation may require some deft facilitation, possibly best done by someone other than the chair of the board. Engaging an external facilitator can be useful where board members are new to the review process, or where they do not know each other well.

Individual conversations

Some boards choose to put individual self-assessment at the heart of their review process. Some may do this formally, with board members preparing their own self-evaluations. Others omit this dimension altogether because it can feel like an uncomfortable and personal appraisal process.

There are ways to make this easier, though. For example, these individual discussions could be part of an annual cycle of conversations between individual board members and the chair, held at the start and the end of each year. They might cover basic matters such as meeting attendance and level of contribution. But to be really useful, the discussions should provide an opportunity to talk about *how* the individual contributes, the balance of challenge and support in their comments, as well as the working relationships they have built with executives and other members of the board.

This may work best as part of a mutual feedback process, with members both receiving feedback from the chair, as well as offering it. As in any context, feedback needs to be triangulated, but a good process can foster the self-awareness of individual board members, helping them to manage their contribution for best effect.

Sometimes, though, the conversation needs to address a *lack* of appropriate contribution. The chair must address these issues, however painful the conversation might be; unless they are tackled, board conversations will be less effective, and may even damage working relationships. Unhelpful behaviour from just one board member makes it harder for the rest of the board to contribute effectively; for example, someone who challenges at length on trivial matters consumes time in the meeting, preventing discussion of more significant topics.

Actions as an outcome

Since all these review conversations – both formal or informal – should generate some actions, the board should also reflect on the actions they agreed previously, to be sure that they have been implemented and to consider whether they have made any difference.

Case study: Taking a different approach

The annual board review showed clearly what everyone had known for some time: boardroom conversations were not effective, either in oversight mode or in collaborative conversations about strategy. Too many discussions ended with unclear decisions or no conclusions at all because the views of board members differed so widely; contributions from some board members appeared to be ignored and there was never enough time to reach a workable compromise in discussion.

After a round of individual conversations with each board member, the chair decided to take a different approach – commissioning a workshop, with an external facilitator, to look at data about board members' psychometric preferences. This data generated some very different conversations, as board members learnt more about their various styles and approaches. They gained a level of respect for each other, a degree of psychological safety and a recognition that their different views could be useful rather than destabilizing. As a result, board members were more willing to listen and consider other views, making agreement easier to achieve.

Summary

- Boards should not miss the opportunity for conversations about their own effectiveness; it is valuable and many regulatory codes suggest that it is mandatory.
- Benefits include the exchange of views on their collective performance, improvements in board efficiency, and the surfacing of any issues.
- There is a range of options about the effectiveness review process in scope and style.
- Boards will want to define a process that works for their particular context, combining the two key ingredients – data and conversation.
- Individual board member reviews based on self-evaluation are an opportunity for mutual feedback.

Checklist: Reviewing board effectiveness – choices for the board

Option	Option
Informal in style (e.g., casual conversations about what went well and what could be better).	Formal, with data collected in advance.
Regular (e.g., a conversation at the end of a board meeting).	Scheduled/annual (e.g., at an annual board workshop).
Internal involving only members of the board, or members of the organization.	External – led by an external reviewer and facilitator.
Involving internal reflection only.	Including an element of benchmarking or comparison with other boards.
Focused at the board level collectively.	Including individual reviews with each member of the board, led by the chair.

Option	Option
Built around self-evaluation by each member of the board about their own contribution and their view of the board's work.	Built around evaluations of the board's collective performance only.
Involving a degree of peer feedback, so that each board member reflects on the contribution of every other board member.	Including feedback on the contribution of the chair as part of their individual review.

With the CEO:
Coaching, confiding, challenging

The conversations between independent board members and the most senior executive in the organization are key to the board's effectiveness. The term CEO is used here to denote this role, although in other sectors, the title will be different – for example, Principal, Managing Partner, or Head Teacher.

Whatever the title, the most senior executive leader in an organization is a key player in an effective board. Typically, that person will interact most frequently with the chair of the board, as described in *Conversation 3: About chairing*. A sound working relationship between each of the independent board members and the CEO brings benefits all round and makes for better governance.

Board members and CEOs typically engage in three different styles of conversation, either inside or outside the boardroom: coaching, confiding and challenging. These are two-way conversations that are useful to *both* the CEO and the board members. They work best as part of good working relationships, so this framework also assumes that there will be opportunities for independent board members to observe and work with the CEO. And those observations may then also feed into the CEO performance appraisal process, as described below.

Three styles of conversation

Figure 11.1 illustrates the three kinds of mutually beneficial conversations between independent board members and the CEO.

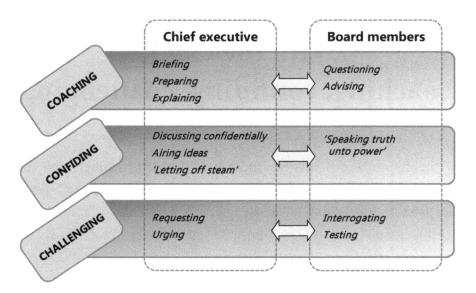

Figure 11.1   Conversations between the CEO and board members

Real interactions may not fit neatly into one or other category, but the figure poses the question: *Do you have all three types of conversation – and, if not, what might the board be missing?*

Each of these types of conversation adds to the value of the board's work. If they are not mutual – if they don't work both ways – the benefits are reduced, for the CEO, for the independent board members and for the board as a whole.

Coaching

Some board conversations might be described as coaching conversations because they are about exploring issues with deft questioning, to generate a better solution. Most importantly, these conversations are about encouraging the CEO to develop a way forward and ensuring that the initiative for action remains with the executive.

The mutual coaching role is evident when the CEO briefs the board and then asks them to reflect on the implications for the organization. For example, the CEO may say in a board meeting: '*The changes in our market make this initiative urgent. I would like to tell you what I learnt at the industry conference, but also explore what we as a board should do about it*'. Board members are in coaching mode, too: the trick here is not to dive in and 'tell' the CEO what to do next. It is to listen, reflect and help them to think through and articulate the next steps.

Good CEOs will invest a great deal of time in briefing board members about what's happening in the organization and outside. Their role requires an understanding of both the external context as well as the organization's internal ability to respond. Many board members comment on the value of such briefings because it helps them to avoid trying to apply 'old' solutions from their previous experience to this new context.

But these aren't just generic briefings – rather, they help the board to move to action. One interviewee talked about the value of the briefing from the CEO: '*The mood music emerging from the regulator meant that we needed to set much more ambitious targets in this area, even though the cost–benefit justification had not been proven. Understanding this in real time helped us develop our plans more quickly*'.

CEOs use a range of methods to keep independent board members informed, such as:

- a regular informal email giving a summary of current issues;
- time spent before and after the board meeting talking informally;
- a regular session with each independent board member, at least annually;
- specific briefing workshops on key topics.

The information exchange should work both ways. Just as the CEO helps board members to learn, board members have insights, experience and networks to offer. For example, it may be appropriate for a board member to lead a board briefing because of particular areas of expertise.

However, in reality, sometimes the conversation is one-sided: many independent board members say that the skills that made them attractive at appointment are largely under-exploited once they are in post. This may be because the CEO wants to feel self-sufficient, or is concerned about losing control. Or it may be because the CEO feels that the experience being offered is insufficiently attuned to the specific circumstances of the organization.

The better the working relationship with the CEO, the easier it is to have constructive, two-way conversations. And the onus is on independent board members to understand the organization well enough to contribute; this starts with their induction process, as described in *Conversation 5: About the organization*, but they also need to keep up to date throughout their tenure. In meetings, board members will want to ask questions for clarification, to make sure that they have understood the proposal or decision – for example: '*What other options did you consider?*'

Independent board members do have advice to offer, although, as this book emphasizes, it has to be offered carefully. For example, '*I have seen this kind of problem before and it can be hard to resolve quickly, so can we discuss this further?*' is probably more useful than '*Let me tell you what happened the last time I saw a situation like this*'.

Because they have a collective responsibility to make the board work effectively, all board members can and should have conversations in a coaching style, each offering insights to the other – and this should include the CEO, even where they are not formally a member of the board. These mutual, coaching-style conversations lay the foundations for sound working relationships, but, although they may be courteous, they can't be cosy. Coaching is not just about support; it is about challenge too, and encouraging the other person in the conversation to reflect and retain ownership of the problem and the solution.

Confiding

Understanding what is on the CEO's mind – what's keeping them awake at night – helps board members to do their job.

Sometimes, these may be matters that the CEO cannot discuss inside the organization because of reporting lines: for example, issues about performance, redundancies, or possible mergers. Conversations with independent board members can be a safe and confidential space for the CEO to talk about key issues with people who understand the context but who can be objective. CEOs report that the space to think out loud can be extremely helpful, even when the independent board member simply serves as a listening ear.

There is a second benefit for the CEO: these confidential conversations are the space for independent board members to provide unvarnished information about what they have observed in the organization. Newly appointed CEOs discover that, as the most senior leader in the organization, the information they receive is filtered – not necessarily for malicious reasons, but perhaps out of anxiety. Some CEOs encourage this, consciously or unconsciously: an intemperate reaction to bad news trains the organization to relay only good news. Independent board members can play a vital role reflecting back their observations to the CEO without value judgements. This 'speaking truth unto power' requires care, but good CEOs find it invaluable.

Sometimes these conversations might stray into a private discussion of the CEO's performance. However, the key thing to remember as an independent board member is that you are not the person running the organization. Providing a running commentary on how the CEO is performing is not part of the role. Providing feedback is sometimes described as a 'gift', but it may be returned unopened if the CEO is not ready to receive it. These matters may best be handled in a scheduled performance appraisal process, as described later in this conversation.

Challenging

Good working relationships round the boardroom table involve challenge as well as support. These two come in various forms, and what is appropriate challenge in one context may not be in another. But the dynamic between the CEO and the board, particularly the independent board members, must allow different views to be expressed in an open debate.

Independent board members are often advised to blend challenge and support in their conversations with the executive. But CEOs challenge boards, too – perhaps with ambitious plans: 'We *simply have to do this!*' This particular sentence often makes board members nervous, challenging them to agree to something that may not have been as rationally argued as they might like. Or the CEO may respond strongly to the board's challenge: '*I take your point, but I don't think the organization is ready to do this now, because of other priorities*'.

CEOs sometimes report that they are frustrated by the lack of ambition and the level of risk aversion from their board. This is not surprising, given the series of high-profile governance disasters that have occurred in almost every sector. Such conflicts are better explored openly, with the CEO challenging the board's views. Otherwise, there may be a temptation to leave some important items off the board agenda and proceed under the board's radar, on the grounds that '*we will never get this through the board*'.

And board members will want to challenge, asking searching questions and testing proposals: for example, '*This looks like a good idea, but can you really get it done in time for September?*' They may raise particular concerns: '*This feels more risky to me than the paper suggests it is...*' – or express a more general challenge about the strategic opportunities that are being overlooked.

Conversations like these won't always be comfortable, but this kind of constructive dialogue is a key part of good governance.

Building working relationships

There are two questions every independent board member will ask themselves about the CEO – and the CEO will also be asking about them:

1. Do I respect this person?
2. Can I trust this person?

To answer these questions, independent board members should not miss the opportunity of seeing the CEO in action, to get a sense of what kind of leader they are. This understanding is a good basis for a working relationship and it helps with the board's oversight of the organization.

The ideal opportunity is one that allows you to get to know the CEO and which also serves a practical purpose in the organization. That is good use of your time, and theirs. Here are some examples of such opportunities:

- **joining a short-life working group:**   This can be a spin-off activity from the main board, with a subset of the board taking on a particular task with a remit to bring it back to the board for a final decision. Such groups can have various configurations but are a good opportunity to work alongside colleagues from both inside and outside the boardroom.
- **partnering with an area of the business:**   Pairing board members with specific functional areas, subsidiaries or business units offers the opportunity to understand the business in more detail. However, board members should avoid becoming so attached to their allocated area that they are seen to advocate on their behalf or adopt a quasi-executive role. It's useful

to generate some rules of engagement in conversation, so that everyone understands what happens and why.

- **attending stakeholder events:** Joining or listening in to stakeholder meetings offers a good opportunity to see the CEO in action.
- **listening in to executive meetings:** This is a rich opportunity to understand how the organization is being managed, but should not be a regular activity because it tempts board members to delve into operational detail and may constrain executives.

These are occasions to see at first hand how the executive team work together under the leadership of the CEO.

CEO performance appraisals

These observations might feed into a formal appraisal process for the CEO, often led by the chair. Such arrangements will differ depending on the context; in some sectors, for example, the increase in financial value of the organization or share price is taken as the primary, even sole, measure of performance. In other contexts, board members may be invited to contribute to 360-degree feedback or to a formal stakeholder review process. Often these conversations happen between the chair and the CEO, but the wider the range of views from board members and stakeholders, the better the process.

Any such contributions need to be based on observation of the CEO's performance inside the boardroom and outside, and the checklist at the end of this conversation sets out some areas to consider.

Performance appraisals work best when there is a clear and agreed set of measures or objectives for the evaluation. This includes being explicit about the assumptions the board is making about how the CEO will behave, as the case study illustrates.

Case study: Developing a shared understanding

The board appointed a new CEO to initiate a substantial review of strategy and to build a new top team to implement it, in the face of competitive pressure and an unsustainable cost base. Although the CEO did spend time on this set of priorities, he also took on a non-executive role in an organization facing similar pressures, in a different sector. These two roles together required extensive international travel, and independent board members began to complain that they did not see enough of the CEO in their own head office, doing the job they had appointed him to do.

The board had failed make clear their expectations at the recruitment stage, and had not agreed 'ground rules' at the outset. As a result, the working relationship between the CEO and the independent board members steadily worsened. Eventually, the CEO resigned, because the relationship could not be rebuilt and the board had to rerun the recruitment process to find a new CEO.

Summary

- Conversations with the CEO or senior executive leader in any organization matter to the chair and to independent board members, as a source of *mutual* benefit.
- They take various forms:
  - *Coaching:* Conversations in which the CEO may provide information or guidance to board members, and they may offer experience or expertise in return. Questioning and advising are key ingredients in the discussions.
  - *Confiding:* These conversations allow the CEO to discuss confidential issues that can't be talked about inside the organization or in the boardroom, while the independent board

members can 'speak truth unto power', offering unvarnished information that may not have reached the CEO.

- ◻ *Challenging:* A degree of mutual challenge is necessary round the boardroom table, expressing members' different perspectives, in order to make wise decisions in complex circumstances.
- These conversations work best in the context of good working relationships, and independent board members should seize opportunities to observe the CEO in action, by participating in working groups, attending stakeholder events, or listening in to executive meetings.
- These observations will help board members to contribute to the formal performance appraisal of the CEO, if they are given the opportunity to do so.

Checklist: Observing the CEO's performance

Questions for observation
Where does the CEO spend their time? Is the balance of time spent on internal matters or engaging externally – and is this appropriate given where the organization is now?
How does the CEO model the values of the organization in their own behaviour? For example, do they have a large separate office guarded from the rest of the organization or do they work mostly in open-plan work areas with other managers and staff?
Does the CEO have a compelling vision for the organization?
Can the CEO articulate the strategy, talk about how it connects to the organization's purpose, and set out their role in turning this into reality?
How does the leadership team work together? Is there mutual support within the team or do they compete with each other?
How is the leadership team organized? Does the structure allow each member to focus appropriately on their role and yet to co-ordinate their activities?
Does the leadership team have the right set of skills? Has the CEO recruited outstanding people or compromised on appointments?

With staff:
Talking and listening to
those who work here

Board membership is a leadership role and real engagement with members of the organization is now regarded as *vital* for an effective board. After all, staff are key stakeholders for any organization, as discussed in *Conversation 9: About people and reward*.

Engagement with employees used to be viewed as a job for management, not for board members, because of their different responsibilities. But talking to staff gives you the chance to see how the organization's strategies are being implemented, and whether key messages from the board are being heard. These conversations are in reality part of the board's role in overseeing what actually happens, rather than what the board has decided should happen. And members of staff report that they appreciate visits from board members, and are reassured to see that there is an understanding of the organization's work at board level. But these arrangements must also include staff who work part-time or remotely.

Many governance codes emphasize the importance of this interaction: for example, provision 5 of the UK Corporate Governance Code for companies reminds boards of the importance of hearing the 'employee voice'.[44]

There are different ways in which board members can talk with – and, importantly, listen to – members of staff in the organization. The ideas here will help you to talk so that staff feel like listening – and listen so that staff feel comfortable to talk.

Preparing

As a board member, you should be aware of the way in which the organization communicates to, and hears back from, members of staff – staff communication channels, feedback mechanisms and staff engagement or opinion surveys. Such data should come to the board in some form, as emphasized in *Conversation 9: About people and reward*, because this is part of the organization's responsibility to these key stakeholders.[45]

Finding the right opportunity

In an era of hybrid working, with many members of staff working remotely, it can be hard to find ways to meet staff in person. To avoid the 'state-visit', in which you only see selected areas of the organization, find an opportunity that is already in the organizational calendar: for example, a team meeting, an away-day, an in-service education and training (INSET) day in a UK school, or the annual start-of-year meeting. These existing events allow you to meet and listen to groups of staff in a setting which is more natural for them.

Some organizations set up specific occasions for staff to meet with board members – informal lunches on board meeting days, or staff joining part of a board meeting as an observer, during their induction. You might also find that there is a formal workforce advisory panel, or a shadow board made up of members of staff whom you might meet. And conversations in the margins of board meetings may give you the chance to talk to staff who have come to present on a specific agenda item.

Social events can be opportunities, too – either run by the board, or in which board members participate. One organization held a charity baking competition and asked the board to serve as the judging panel, a good chance for informal interaction. Such events sometimes require the board to step outside their comfort zones: a 'guess-the-baby' photo competition might not be the way you want to present yourself to members of staff, but it is the taking part that counts.

Contributing

Participating in organizational initiatives allows independent board members to learn more about what's happening inside, as well as adding some value. For example, active involvement in succession planning for senior and high-talent staff helps the organization and lends weight to the board's oversight. This might involve being a panel member in an assessment centre, serving as a mentor for a member of staff, or participating in development events. The challenge here is, of course, to maintain the independence of your view, and the boundary of your role, but board member involvement in such activities can bring to life the board's responsibility for proper resourcing of the organization.

Talking and listening

These occasions will allow you to listen, and to learn how members of staff are feeling about the organization or about specific issues. The balance of talking and listening for you should probably be roughly 30:70 – spending around 30% of the time explaining your role, the reasons for your visit and asking questions, and listening attentively for the rest of the time.

When you talk with members of staff, do you feel that they are able to speak freely? Does the head of the function or team allow you to meet with members of staff on your own, or do they prefer to be present, too? Setting up the conversation properly also involves reassuring organizational leaders: they may be anxious that such conversations could bypass normal communication channels and reporting lines, or feel that their own role may be undermined.

In conversations with staff, you are listening out for themes, which the board may have discussed, for cultural indicators or for those aspects of the way the organization works that are problematic for staff. For example, in one organization centralized photocopying was introduced as a way to save money on copiers and exercise tighter controls. But staff felt this was unrealistic: to them, the cost of delay and the time involved was greater than any apparent saving. It was not the board member's job to solve that issue, but these views did make the board consider testing future changes in one part of the organization before implementing them everywhere.

Observing

To do the board role well, you can't be disconnected from the reality of what happens in the organization. Your conversations with staff give you the chance to learn whether the board's view of events is matched by the view from staff. You can test your assumptions about the organization's culture: look for the rituals, symbols and routines inside the organization, which tell you more about the real culture of the organization than the framed statements about values. For example, in one organization, car parking spaces were allocated according to organizational hierarchy rather than individual need, and plants were provided for each workspace on the basis of seniority. While there may be logic to some of these arrangements, they are also clues about what – or who – the organization really values. The *Introduction* to this book offers a framework to help you to do this, the culture web.

During your visits, concentrate on observing, not making judgements, using the kind of ethnographer's approach also described in the *Introduction*. For example, when governors visit schools, as is encouraged by the regulator, they often report back using a written template, which gets them to focus purely on what they see. Since governors are often not trained teachers, it is not for them to interpret and evaluate; nor would this necessarily be well received by staff, because these are not inspection visits. But such visits do help school governors to answer the key question: '*How do you know?*' If you have seen that the policies and practices you have agreed at the board level are being used in the organization, that's the answer.

Discussing problems

Sometimes, staff may take the opportunity to raise a particular concern with you – and this is precisely the situation that can make executive leaders nervous. Most organizations have proper processes to deal with grievances or complaints, and conversation with a board member runs the risk of by-passing those carefully designed processes. So, if this happens in your conversations with staff, the first thing to do is to ask whether or not they have been able to discuss the issue with their line manager or with the HR team.

As a board member, it is not your role to resolve such issues. You may not have understood the situation fully, or there may be other people involved who see the situation differently. It can therefore be hard to demonstrate that you are listening, because you cannot offer a solution. All you can do is to acknowledge this as part of the conversation, explaining your role as clearly as possible.

Following up

You may well want to ask questions to follow up on what you have been told, or what you have seen. These subsequent conversations require care, so that executive leaders do not feel caught out or undermined. You are looking for the opportunity to understand the situation from a wider perspective, rather than a forensic dissection of the particular issue raised by one individual. The case study that follows towards the end of this conversation gives an example of this situation.

Talking with the board secretary

The secretary to the board – or clerk in other contexts – is a key person for board members to interact with and may often be a member of staff, although not always. Some boards employ someone specifically to take this role, or even outsource it, but if the board secretary is a member of staff, that person may be able to help board members to get a sense of staff reactions – even if the role is not formally a staff liaison role. But it is worth remembering that they may not have their finger on the pulse of the organization and their view may not be representative.

Talking with a staff board member

Some organizations have a member of staff serving on the board, in addition to their day job. This is a role that can be defined in various ways, and there is more about this in *Conversation 13: With stakeholders*. The board can benefit greatly from hearing at first hand the views from a member of staff, provided that the person appointed to the role understands its scope, is offered some training, and has appropriate support to do it alongside their day job.

Case study: Listening to staff views

An independent board member at a major university took the opportunity to talk to the security guards when he arrived early for a meeting. In the course of the conversation, he heard about the problems that often arose late on Sunday evenings. International students arriving after long journeys for the start of term, or short courses, often wanted to check in to their accommodation late at night. The security team found this hard to handle because they only intermittently served on reception and did not have access to the right systems.

Rather than bringing this to the board as an issue, the board member followed up by asking questions – meeting the director of student services to talk about arrangements for new students in general and residential arrivals in particular. This served as an exploratory conversation intended to understand the situation from a wider perspective, and not board interference in specific operational matters.

Summary

- Board membership is a leadership role, and engagement with employees is vital.
- Board members need to understand whether the board's view of the organization matches the reality of what happens in the organization, observing without judgement.
- Participating in existing events or activities or contributing to working groups is a useful way to be involved.
- Conversations with members of staff work better with more listening than talking – perhaps in the ratio of 30% talking to 70% listening, as a rough guide.
- Board members always need to triangulate what they see and hear during these visits, with other information, in order to understand the situation as fully as possible.

Checklist: Questions for reflection

Questions for reflection
What are the opportunities to meet staff in the organization – for example, working groups, staff forums, development activities, social events or celebrations?
Can we contribute to organizational activities, such as recruitment panels?

Questions for reflection
Do we as board members agree between us a schedule of visits, so we balance our involvement across a range of functions and events?
When we visit the organization, are we accompanied and taken to specific areas or are we able to talk to any member of staff?
What sort of feedback do we give after each visit?

With stakeholders: Developing a stakeholder mindset

Boards in every sector increasingly talk both *with* and *about* their stakeholders. Regulators expect this, and some also require that the organization demonstrates how stakeholder views have been taken into account when developing strategy. These are important conversations, but it's easy to miss the point: it's not so much about stakeholder management, but more having a stakeholder *mindset*. It is not just about engaging with them but also about bringing their perspective into the boardroom. This new emphasis comes from a wider sense of social and environmental interconnectedness and shifts in society's attitudes to what can and should be done by organizations.

Stakeholders

The collective noun refers to any group or individual who can affect, or is affected by, the achievement of the organization's objective. These might be internal – such as employees – or external, including customers, suppliers and regulators as well as shareholders.

Stakeholder theory is based on the premise that a firm should create value for all stakeholders, not just shareholders.[46]

The interconnectedness of relationships between a business and its various stakeholders implies that the organization – and, therefore, the board – should be engaged with stakeholders, and understand their issues and perspectives. There is growing attention to these issues in the UK, manifest in the focus on ESG (environmental, social and governance) matters.

Social licence to operate

Increasingly, in almost every sector, boards are accountable for creating sustainable value for wider society, not just for their shareholders. Taking a stakeholder approach is becoming part of the social licence to operate, or 'SLO'. This refers to the continuing acceptance of an organization's standard business practices and operating procedures granted by its employees, stakeholders and the general public. Organizations will earn an SLO over time by building trust with all its stakeholders. In order to protect and build social licence, organizations are encouraged to first do the right thing and then to be seen doing the right thing.

Stakeholder capitalism

The combination of the health pandemic, the cost-of-living crisis, social movements such as Black Lives Matter, as well as the threats from climate change have raised the requirements for business to address inequality and social justice, while still achieving returns for shareholders. This is known as *stakeholder capitalism* and this broadening remit for business has moved beyond corporate institutional investors and is influencing the thinking in not-for-profit and public-sector settings also.

Institutional investors examine how companies deal with medium-to long-term risks posed by climate change, as well as their focus on social justice. They look closely at diversity, equity and inclusion policies, as well as engagement with staff, and at their range of responsible business practices, to be sure that long-term sustainable planning is happening in the boardroom.

Regulatory requirements

In the private sector in the UK, the definition of a director's duty includes '*the need to foster the company's business relationships with suppliers, customers and others*' and to consider '*the impact of the company's operations on the community and the environment*'.[47] This approach has its detractors, with commentators asking whether the new regulatory emphasis is anything more than window dressing; they point to examples of 'green-washing' from corporates as well as 'purpose-washing'. There are others who feel that all this is an unnecessary distraction from the task of creating a profitable business.

In other sectors, there are similar regulatory requirements. For example, the UK Charity Governance Code Principle 7 (Openness and Transparency) requires the board to communicate and consult effectively with stakeholders with an interest in the charity's work, including users, beneficiaries, staff, volunteers, donors, suppliers, local communities and others.[48] Likewise, the governance code for higher education institutions also includes the requirement that: '*Governing Bodies understand the various stakeholders of the institution globally, nationally and locally and are assured that appropriate and meaningful engagement takes place to allow stakeholder views to be considered and reflected in relevant decision-making processes*'.[49]

Developing a stakeholder mindset

Apart from the regulatory and social necessity to consider stakeholders, there are benefits for boards in developing a stakeholder mindset. This is not simply about stakeholder mapping, or stakeholder engagement, although both are clearly integral – and often undervalued – in 21st-century organizations. Rather, it is about consistent, informed attention to stakeholders and their issues and perspectives as part of the board's oversight. There is real value to be had from these conversations, and considerable risk if they never happen. Long-term, sustainable success depends to a greater degree on an organization's stakeholders, their attitudes and actions than some boards realize. And both experience and research indicate that the more diverse the board, the better they are likely to be at taking account of the range of stakeholder interests.

A stakeholder mindset will be visible outside the boardroom, too, not only in the time and effort spent in engaging with stakeholders. Purpose statements often refer to a wider group of stakeholders beyond customers or service users. There is evidence that non-financial criteria are becoming more common in CEO compensation packages in the private sector and there has been a clear shift in thinking over shareholder primacy in corporate boardrooms. Charities with a large endowment now pay close attention to where their funds are invested, for example, and donations are scrutinized more carefully.

Strong working relationships with suppliers, customers or service users help an organization to work more effectively with them – and may also help the organization to weather a crisis, since stakeholders may be more willing to offer support or simply tolerance. An organization's reputation really belongs in the eye of the beholder, or stakeholder, so there is a business need to understand their views of your organization.[50]

Identifying and prioritizing stakeholders

While executives may be responsible for direct engagement with stakeholders, board members will want to have in their minds a clear picture of the stakeholder landscape: those who will be materially affected by decisions, those with influence, and the issues they are concerned about. This may involve some stakeholder mapping, but the term 'stakeholder management' implies a greater degree of control over stakeholder relationships than is realistic.

Primary stakeholders are both internal and external and will be easy to identify and probably to engage with. They include customers, as well as service users, students in an educational organization or citizens in a public-sector body. Secondary stakeholders include those with an indirect influence – for example, government agencies, suppliers, and local communities.

With such a wide range, there will obviously need to be some sense of priority, in the time and investment made in engagement activities. It's not always easy to prioritize – and events may change those priorities suddenly, too. Stakeholders may express their concerns publicly at any point – activism is a part of the landscape for all organizations, and social media gives individual views new power and prominence.

Engaging with stakeholders

Engagement with stakeholders is ideally a mutual conversation. It's about both telling and listening, to keep stakeholders informed about what your organization is doing and to learn about their plans, as well as their reactions to yours. This mutual conversation is valuable – for example, it may be that something they plan to do might open up a new opportunity, or become a major threat.

The board will want to take a proportionate approach: stakeholder activity will obviously be very different in a large listed company from a small charity. But the law of inverse governance applies here: the smaller the organization, the more board members will find themselves being pulled into lower levels of detail or more direct engagement with stakeholders.

There are various ways to create opportunities for this mutual conversation. For example, stakeholders who are strategically important to your organization may be connected through partnership agreements and scheduled reviews will create the opportunity for a wider conversation. Stakeholders with strong dependency and influence may be willing to attend open forums or seminars, or may be formally engaged through advisory or user groups. Those with lower levels of dependency and influence may receive regular communications through newsletters or direct mailings, but these are one-sided mechanisms and the board may miss useful insights as a result. This can be countered with internal research, and it also helps if independent board members are active externally, finding opportunities to meet and hear from stakeholders.

Some organizations use a range of ways to engage with their customers – not simply in feedback surveys but in setting up opportunities to co-create or consult with them, for example, as part of new product or service design. For others, such as utilities, regulation requires such interactions.

All these activities can consume considerable time and energy, sometimes with insufficient benefit in terms of relationship-building or learning. But these are not peripheral: they may be both required by the regulator and useful to the board, so they should be on the agenda.

Engaging with staff

Employees are a key stakeholder group in all organizations. *Conversation 12: With staff* focuses on the importance of talking and listening to members of staff, but this Conversation looks at ways of ensuring that their voice is heard in the boardroom. Once again, a stakeholder mindset goes beyond simply attending to the data, such as staff opinion surveys, or sickness and turnover statistics. Some organizations set up a shadow board, allowing members of staff to see most of the same papers that the board sees, to gain a staff perspective on the key issues and decisions.

Others may have staff or service users as board members, involved in the discussions directly. These might be representative roles, in which the individual represents the views of staff and puts them forward in discussion. Or the post might be for a staff-elected member, with no representative role at all. This may, however, present that person with a dilemma: they have joined the board as a member, with all the duties of board members to the organization as a whole, but their colleagues in the organization may be expecting them to operate mainly as a representative of their views. If it is to work well, the definition of the role needs to be clear to all parties.

In the UK private sector, the 2018 Corporate Governance Code now requires listed companies to adopt one (or a combination) of three mechanisms to ensure that the board is actively engaging with employees: a director appointed from the workforce, a workforce advisory panel or a designated non-executive director with specific responsibility to talk with and listen to members of staff. Companies either need to comply with one of these or explain why it considers that the other arrangements they have in place are effective. Whether or not that code applies to your organization, it is well worth considering the arrangements your organization has in place for staff views to be part of boardroom conversations.

Learning

Such engagement and the learning that it generates is strategically useful, so board members will want to be sure that their conversations cover the insights from the activity, not simply what has been done and with whom. This is the moment to use the 'bifocal lens', described in the *Introduction*, to observe the diverse range of stakeholder views clearly.

There are other ways to help the board to remain alert, including allocating independent board members to focus on specific themes or stakeholder groups. Particular issues may be suddenly magnified into major risks, and develop into a crisis – see *Conversation 18: About a crisis* – but it is often too late to respond effectively at that point, so early awareness matters.

Case study: Stakeholder action

In 2019, a number of stakeholders involved in De Montfort University (DMU) based in Leicester in the UK raised serious concerns: members of staff, an anonymous whistle-blower, and the regulator, the Office for Students. In addition, two staff unions, the University and College Union (UCU) and UNISON (a UK public-service union), held a vote of no confidence, and produced a manifesto, 'DMU Renewed', which called for *greater transparency from the university and a "democratisation" that would see staff and students given a greater say in the way top level decisions are made in the future*.[51]

The UK-based Office for Students, as the regulator, led an investigation which found some major issues, including questions about the independence and rigour of remuneration decisions, conflicts of interest and paid consultancy arrangements with members of the board of governors, as well as concerns about the handling of whistle-blowing by the university.

As a result, the university's senior leadership was changed, with the vice-chancellor and the chair of the board of governors departing. The interim vice-chancellor and the new governors undertook a major review of governance arrangements and of the organization's culture: *'The Executive Board has undertaken an extensive engagement with staff and other stakeholders to identify their perspective on the changes required, with a firm commitment to deliver the agreed changes as a priority'*.[52]

Summary

- Boards are increasingly accountable for creating sustainable value for society, not just for shareholders. The interconnections between an organization and its various stakeholders are critical in its operations and to its reputation.
- A stakeholder is any group or individual who can affect, or is affected by, the achievement of the organization's objectives. This includes internal stakeholders (employees) as well as those outside the organization: customers, suppliers, regulators and shareholders.
- Regulators in many sectors expect visible stakeholder engagement, and the 'social licence to operate' is built on the trust between an organization and its stakeholders.
- Stakeholder engagement activities are vital, but these are less about stakeholder management and more about developing a stakeholder mindset in the boardroom: consistent, informed attention to stakeholders and their issues and perspectives as part of the board's oversight.
- Organizations identify both primary and secondary stakeholders, and develop engagement activities to allow mutual conversations, so that the organization learns about stakeholder issues and plans, rather than simply communicating their own plans.
- Hearing the stakeholder voice in the boardroom is part of the stakeholder mindset, and it's particularly important to hear the employee voice. This is not simply about data from staff surveys but more direct engagement with staff.

Checklist: Questions for reflection

Questions for reflection
Which organizations, groups or individuals could be affected by our actions – positively or negatively? And who has strong influence over what the organization does?
How often is the topic of stakeholders discussed at the board and in what context? Do we hear the stakeholder voice in discussions? Does the board have a stakeholder mindset?
What are the methods of engaging with each stakeholder and do they work well?
Do the reports on stakeholder engagement focus entirely on activities or do they also include the insights from them?
Are there any stakeholders the board should meet with directly?

With regulators:
Understanding the relationship

E very organization will be subject to at least one form of regulation, and, in many cases, to more than one. Although this is a complex topic, board members need to be clear about who regulates their activities – why and how – and to talk about how changes in regulatory approaches might affect them.

The frameworks set out here can help the board to understand the relationship with its regulator, or regulators, and serve as a basis for conversations with board colleagues.

Challenges for board members

Regulation brings some specific challenges for board members, particularly independent board members:

- The regulatory burden in the boardroom has increased and its scope and nature are changing in response to environmental and social issues. This is bringing new requirements, such as disclosure of carbon emissions and new targets (e.g., for gender representation on boards).
- Regulators are focusing more on values and culture as important components in an organization's approach. The board has an vital role in this respect, although it is not clear exactly how that role can be regulated.

- Changes in regulation tend to increase the individual accountability of specific roles in the boardroom. Boards are now asked to provide assurance on specific topics, which require much more detailed knowledge of the organization, blurring the lines between executive responsibility and non-executive oversight.
- Independent board members are increasingly required to know more about the way regulatory compliance works in their organization. This can feel particularly burdensome for voluntary roles such as school governors because closer involvement requires more time than many people are able to give.
- Regulatory problems can tarnish the reputations of independent board members, whether justifiably or not. This will affect their ability to take on other roles in future – and search consultants report this as an increasing concern from potential candidates for board roles.

So, how can you, as an independent board member, be clear about your role and the board's role in respect of regulation?

Regulation: The context

First, understand the landscape of regulation. Regulation can take many forms – regulators of professions, economic regulators, or public service regulators, for example. In the UK, government and parliament use regulation to deliver policy objectives, especially in areas where government does not provide or commission services directly.

Regulators set out rules and behaviours that people and organizations are expected to follow. Many organizations are overseen by more than one regulator – some local and some national. Some have the power to influence, and others can enforce compliance. Sometimes, there is no clear boundary between the different regulators because they are not required to work together – rather, it is the board's responsibility to understand their interlocking regulatory roles.

Who regulates you?

Second, therefore, board members need to be clear about who specifically regulates your organization, why and how. Figure 14.1 illustrates the scope and purpose of regulation within the UK, and it will help you to understand their organization's regulatory schedule.

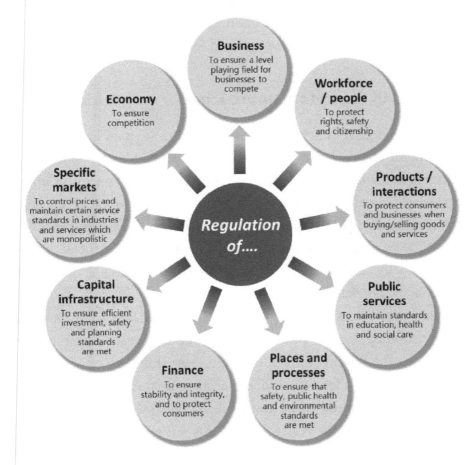

Figure 14.1   Scope and purpose of regulation in the UK

Adapted from the National Audit Office's *A Short Guide to Regulation*

To take one example to illustrate the complexity: a UK water company will be subject to its own regulatory body, Ofwat, as well as the Consumer Council for Water (CCW), The Drinking Water Inspectorate (DWI) regulating the product, the Environment Agency and the Department for Environment, Food and Rural Affairs (DEFRA) in addition to the standard operating regulations that affect all organizations. As a second example, schools are subject to inspection by Ofsted (the Office for Standards in Education, Children's Services and Skills), oversight from the UK Department for Education, as well as regulation by local authorities. Making sense of a multi-regulatory environment won't be easy, but it's vital for good governance to have a clear and shared understanding – hence the need for conversation.

Changes in regulatory approaches

Boards also need to watch out for changes in the way they are regulated. Many of the scandals of the past decades have generated new approaches and regulators have assumed new powers over areas that were previously exclusively board responsibility. For example, the regulation of financial services has changed significantly since the US and global financial scandals of 2008, while the case of Dr Harold Shipman, a UK general practitioner (doctor) and serial killer, was the catalyst for changing the face of professional regulation in the UK.

In other sectors, regulatory changes have been driven by changes in the funding model. For example, in the university sector in the UK, when the funding model for institutions shifted to one in which funding effectively followed individual students through their student loan, the effect on the sector and its regulation was profound. A new regulator known as the Office for Students was set up, with a mandate simply requiring UK universities to register as an appropriate provider, offering no guidance or support.

Regulatory approaches can be illustrated as a pyramid, moving from providing information and education, up to the command-and-control enforcement approach, often precipitated by a crisis in the sector. Figure 14.2a will help you as a board member to understand the range of regulatory approaches affecting your organization and to plot how they may change.

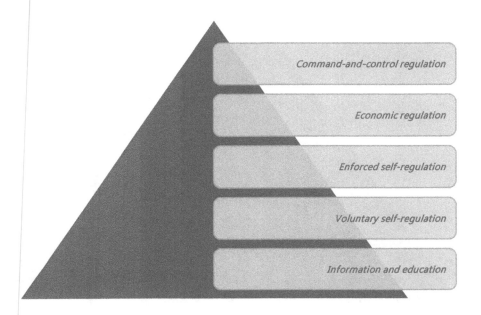

Figure 14.2a   Regulatory approaches

The regulatory approach may move in either direction, up or down this pyramid. For example, funding changes for the UK's Charity Commission prompted a retrenchment in its statutory role: support to trustees was scaled down, and advice became largely web-based. The Commission asked organizations to self-regulate some activities, such as street cash collections, for example, rather than be subject to the Commission's command-and-control approach.

The clues to understanding this are in the kinds of regulatory interventions that you see in your organization. Figure 14.2b gives the same pyramid diagram, but now shows the offers or interventions that a regulator may make.

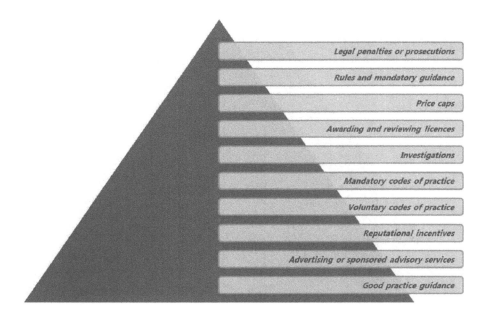

Figure 14.2b   Regulatory actions, offers and interventions

What this means for board members

Some of these changes bring increased responsibilities for board members, blurring the lines between non-executive and executive in uncomfortable ways. For example, in financial services in the UK, the Senior Managers and Certification Regime (SM&CR) was introduced, designed to '*reduce harm to consumers and strengthen market integrity by making individuals more accountable for their conduct and competence*'.[53]

The scheme aims to certify particular role holders as part of their leadership roles of the organizations, covering board roles such as the chair, the senior independent director and the chairs of major board committees. This is a significant shift: in this sector, it marks an increasing expectation that independent directors are viewed as a part of the executive, requiring personal certification and accountability.

If the regulatory approach moves down the pyramid, there will be greater onus on the organization for self-regulation. There are advantages: such changes allow the sector to establish its own regulatory culture and to exert influence on potentially errant members of the sector more directly. But the disadvantages are the additional burden of responsibility and increased workload, particularly for smaller organizations.

A vital board conversation

The board of any organization should talk about the regulatory context in which they work and how it is changing. Compliance in many sectors is business-critical: if your organization is not compliant, even temporarily, you may not be able to continue to operate. Papers on regulation activities will be a regular part of the board pack and organizational resources will be devoted to compliance work, so the board will want to assure itself that this work is effective. That requires any board member to understand what is being regulated and how.

And in strategic planning work, if your organization plans to develop a new product or move into a new market, the board should always ask about the regulatory impact. This can be easy to miss: even the move into a different part of the UK may require the organization to interact with a new regulator, if that responsibility has been devolved from England.

Conversations with the regulator

Increasingly, conversations with the regulators themselves are also part of a board member's responsibility.

Relationships between the regulator and the board – and with independent board members in particular – depend on where in the regulatory pyramid your organization's regulator sits. For example, UK regulator Ofwat expects to engage directly with board members: it meets new appointees and runs a series of non-executive workshops in order to ensure there is a clear understanding of its priorities and to receive feedback from the sector.

And the nature of the relationship at different stages drives different kinds of conversation, each demanding a different focus of attention for the board and the organization.

Stage 1: Stable regulatory environment

In this stage, there is unlikely to be radical change to the regulatory framework, and so regulatory engagement runs to a predictable schedule. However, the board shouldn't forget to look ahead, undertaking some horizon-scanning to establish what social and economic factors might form part of future regulation. What is happening in the sector? Events outside your control can precipitate regulatory changes, as can the actions of a competitor organization.

This stage is also the opportunity for the board to set up some conversations with the relevant regulator. How does the regulator view your organization? Do they trust your governance? Knowing the answers to these questions will help the organization to work more effectively with them.

Stage 2: Regulatory horizon changes

In this phase, as an independent board member, you should expect to be briefed on potential changes, and the changing vision and philosophy behind the proposed regulatory approach. Board members may also have the opportunity to contribute to the thinking and policy work as the regulator formulates their new approach. These are conversations that could have significant influence and they need careful preparation. The UK Financial Reporting Council, for example, has recently set up a Stakeholder Insight Group, offering quarterly meetings, with no agenda, to allow stakeholders to talk about what they actually do, what works and what doesn't. The regulator uses these conversations as a source of learning.

The board will need to stay informed as regulatory changes move from proposal to enactment. At times, this is a demanding task: as an example, during the pandemic, one group of schools allocated a member of the finance team to attend every briefing session from Ofsted, the Department for Education, and legal advisers in the sector to ensure that they were keeping up to date with the frequent changes in regulations necessitated by the global health crisis.

Stage 3: What does it mean for us?

As a board, your conversations at this stage will probably centre on changes in the 'what and how' of regulation. If the proposed changes to the regulatory framework are radical, the board will need assurance that the organization is in shape to deliver against these new regulatory requirements. This may require process alterations, new reporting routines, or a significant shift in attitudes and behaviours. For example, in UK schools, Ofsted inspections now require different data, as the regulatory focus has shifted from outcomes to examine other aspects of the school, such as pupil well-being or ways in which the pupil voice can be heard.

Alternatively, if the changes involve direct regulatory interventions, moving up the pyramid (see Figures 14.2a and 14.2b), board members may need to go through dress rehearsals or mock inspections in preparation and to understand more clearly what is involved.

Stage 4: Direct engagement with the regulator

At this stage, there is very active engagement with the regulator: for example, finalizing a price review with an economic regulator, an inspection, or even a regulatory investigation.

The board needs to be clear about who is doing what and who is talking to whom. If junior staff are involved, they may need support and time to prepare. The board will also benefit from first-hand feedback from those directly engaging with the regulator so that any immediate consequences can be examined, and any necessary actions taken, with proper oversight.

Case study: Good preparation

One financial services organization was contacted by the regulator in response to concerns raised by a whistle-blower. The regulatory framework required that this type of concern be investigated, because there is usually more to the issue than is immediately obvious. In preparation for the regulatory visit, staff were briefed by the board's compliance director to be sure to provide all the information that might be needed, in advance, so that the regulatory team could work through their investigation without hindrance. Some members of the board also re-took some compliance training modules which they had previously completed, to be sure that they were well prepared for their interviews.

The investigation was searching, and took several days. But the atmosphere of openness and the organization's approach to the issue made the process both more efficient and effective. In the end, the regulator was satisfied that no further sanctions would be needed given the organization's clear willingness to take on recommendations for improvement.

Summary

- Board members need to understand the regulatory frameworks they must operate in: who regulates what aspect of the organization and how.
- Regulatory approaches change over time, precipitated by crises, funding alterations or business shifts, including:
  - A closer focus on accountability of roles and individuals in organizations;
  - Attempts to regulate culture and values of boards;
  - A transfer of some of the regulatory burden from the regulator to the sector or to individual organizations;
  - Altered relationships between the regulator and the regulated.
- As an independent board member, there are conversations you need to have to:
  - Understand regulation in your organization;
  - Appreciate the shifting nature of your regulatory landscape.
- Assess what sort of 'regulatory shape' your organization is in.
- Assimilate any specific changing requirements for you in terms of your accountability.
- There are four different stages in any organization's relationship with a regulator, each demanding a different focus of attention for the board and the organization concerned:
  - Stage 1: Stable regulatory environment;
  - Stage 2: Regulatory horizon;
  - Stage 3: Assessing implications;
  - Stage 4: Regulatory intervention.

Checklist: Four stages of engagement with a regulator – activities and outcomes

Stage	Activities/conversations	Outcomes
Stable regulatory framework – no current engagement with the regulator.	Horizon-scanning: keeping up to date with: • regulatory issues and actions elsewhere in the sector; • from other regulators; • competitor intelligence.	Informed conversations in the boardroom and outside.
	Internal discussions with compliance contacts – do we know what our regulators are currently focused on and concerned about?	Informed conversations in the boardroom and outside.
	Relationship mapping, relationship building: low-level engagement with the regulator to build trust.	Efficient working relationship: knowing who to call. Improved mutual understanding of: • who does what in the regulator; • their understanding of what we do.
Regulatory changes being proposed.	Discussion: • How are we involved in and contributing to the proposals about changed regulatory frameworks? • What has caused the changes? • How significant are the changes – scope and scale?	Understanding the changes in the regulator's approach. Contribution to the changed approach.

Stage	Activities/conversations	Outcomes
Regulatory changes being proposed.	Assessing the implications for the board and directors, executive and independent: • Do we understand the new approach (not just ticking new boxes)? • Do sufficient channels exist? • Transparency of the approach?	
	Keeping in touch with the regulator – at the right level and often enough.	Open discussions with the regulator so they can see our preparations.
Organizational response to regulatory change or when regulatory interaction likely.	Overseeing programmes of change to ensure readiness: • role of the board in oversight and contribution (e.g., specific agenda items); • capacity of regulatory function.	Capacity and competence for the new regulatory regime.
	Keeping in touch with the regulator: • Information exchange; • Notifiable events. Discussion: do the right systems exist to create awareness (not just compliance systems)?	Regular constructive contact.

Stage	Activities/conversations	Outcomes
Direct interaction with the regulator.	Rehearsals, including attention to tone and language. Identification of risk areas.	Successful regulatory outcome.
	Possibly: challenging the outcome; whether to challenge; who challenges, how and when.	
	Communicating the outcome to internal and external stakeholders.	

With advisers:
Finding the support
the board needs

Boards use external advisers in various ways: to complete regular and required work, such as the annual audit, or for advice on particular topics, or as a source of additional resources to get something done. The adviser may be contracted for a number of years, as in the audit relationship, or it may be a one-off commission. But in every case, the quality of the board's conversation about the work to be done will make a difference to the value that the organization gets for its expenditure.

There are some key conversations that the board should have before, during and after any work being done by an external organization: in commissioning it, and in reviewing what has been done. These include the statutory conversations that organizations may have with external auditors, as well as the extra-value conversations with advisers at any point during their work.

The commissioning conversation

When there is a discussion about using external advisers to complete a piece of work, the conversation round the boardroom table should help the board to be clear about three particular questions:

1. What outcome do we want from this piece of work?
2. What will we do with the results?
3. Who, precisely, is the client?

The board will use the answers to shape the commission, the brief that is the basis for the adviser's work.

The outcome

Is the board looking for an answer, or for validation of a decision the board has already decided to take? Does the organization simply need to buy in extra pairs of hands with particular skills? Alternatively, is this piece of work a regulatory requirement, but could also become a source of extra value to this organization if set up properly? Or, is the board really looking for generalized reassurance – and, if so, is this the right use of time and resources to get the certainty that external advisers are rarely willing to deliver?

Figure 15.1 summarizes the types of outcome the board may want, simply as a way of underlining the options. And, of course, they are not mutually exclusive: there is often the opportunity to gain more than one type of outcome.

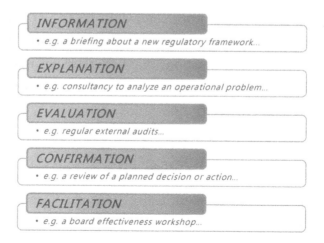

Figure 15.1   The range of outcomes from advisers' work

Using the results

Next, what does the board plan to do with the answers or results from the work? The answer to that question reminds the board of the cost–benefit analysis: how much are we prepared to pay for this outcome? Will we get sufficient value from this commission?

The client for the work

Finally, being clear about exactly who is the client for the work helps to establish the right reporting lines. External advisers may, for example, see the financial director as the client, because they most often work within finance, but the board may be seeking answers that lie outside the finance function, or even affect its work. In that case, the board will want to specify that the report on the work comes directly to the chair of the board. Alternatively, if the adviser is engaged to look at an internal organizational issue, the detailed report will come to the executive responsible, and the board does not need to be engaged in the process, but simply receive the final report.

Shaping the commission

Clear answers to these questions, drawn from board discussion, will help the board to be an 'intelligent customer', packaging the work appropriately, in terms of time, cost and reporting lines. For example, if the board frames the brief as 'we want a view from the lawyers on this topic', the commission may be larger, more expensive and less useful than it needs to be.

If the work is simply to confirm the viability of a decision that the board has already made, or to confirm that an option should be ruled out, the more sharply focused it is, the better. It will take less time, and probably be more cost-effective. But sometimes, the commissioned work has a wider scope, and is deliberately left more open, to see if the advisers come up with something that the board has not considered.

Often, the ideal commission is a blend of the two: for example, if the board is considering a move into a new geography, and commissions a *general* market survey in advance of the decision, what it receives may be too general to be useful. Adding some specific questions to the brief increases the likelihood that the commission will help the board to make the right decision, and it will certainly help the external advisers to do their job more effectively.

Boards will want to be careful, though, about commissioning external advisers to review the work of other external advisers – consultants reviewing the work done by other consultants. This is sometimes done in the search for increased assurance, although the outcome is rarely as definite as you might have hoped. But here, too, the clearer you are about the questions to be answered, what you will do with the results of the work and who is the client for the work, the better.

The review conversation

When the conclusions of the work come to the board for review, the conversation must address the question: Did we get what we asked for? And, if not, why not and how might we still get it? The answer may be some further work, or simply a second conversation with the adviser, more closely structured around some key questions.

Statutory conversations

Almost all boards will have regular conversations with the audit team as part of the annual audit process. These will be part of a multi-year working relationship with the audit firm, but often with an annual commissioning conversation about the scope of the audit work for the year ahead.

This is a vital relationship: auditors can be seen as 'the critical friends of the critical friends' on the board. Unfortunately, this regular item on the agenda for an audit committee or board can often be formulaic in style, with a boiler-plate presentation pack and a rapid, sometimes superficial, review of what the audit team has found. But the board shouldn't miss the opportunity for a more searching conversation with the audit team. If the board can ask the right questions – some examples follow here and the checklist at the end of this *Conversation* – they may well find that there is more value to be had from these advisers, particularly after their work is complete.

Much of the discussion at the audit meeting will be internally focused, looking at particular risk areas, or recommendations for changes. Here, it is always worth asking the follow-up questions: for example, are there alternative changes we might make, other than those you have recommended? What do other organizations do in this area?

Sometimes the recommendations look like a restatement of the problem, as if it were the solution, and the board conversation should press the external team for more information and insight. Has the team really got to the heart of the problem? For example, after one audit, the team noted that '*payment receipt processing is not as timely as it should be, so there needs to be an improved receipt process*'. It transpired that, in reality, the process itself worked well, but a key member of staff in the team had taken advantage of the organization's new flexi-time arrangements, and started work each day at 10.30 in the morning, thus completing the work too late for that day's banking deposit process. This only came to light because one independent board member had seen this situation in another organization and asked the right question.

There is much to be learnt from a more searching conversation in these formal agenda items, if the board and the team are well-prepared. Signalling in advance to the advisers that board members will want to ask a range of questions increases the chances that the advisers will be prepared and will have brought the right people to the discussion.

Private conversations with independent members

Regulatory guidance in the UK states that independent members of the board should have a private discussion with the audit team as they complete their work, and an annual review. This might be as part of a full board meeting, or solely with members of the audit committee. Too often, this is a short and cursory discussion, but once again, if the independent members of the board have some good questions to ask – see the checklist below – the conversation may be more revealing than the audit presentation has been. It can be too easy to waste this opportunity, if the meeting is focused on the statutory task, rather than the opportunity to have an honest, wide-ranging conversation with the audit team.

Extra value conversations

It is worth asking the 'What else?' question: what else has the adviser noticed during their work with the organization and would like to comment on? Get them to reflect on the work they have done with the organization: is there anything else they think the board should know? It is always interesting to see how advisers respond to this question because it gives them the opportunity to demonstrate the depth and breadth of their analysis. Of course, it is also an opportunity for them to talk about further work, which may or may not be of interest to the board at this point.

External advisers have insights into what other organizations do, which, without impropriety, can be useful to board members. Asking open questions about the adviser's view of your particular sector, and the threats and opportunities that might lie ahead, can be revealing. The advisers may even have insights from completely different sectors, drawn from the range of their work.

But the conversation could be even more useful if you are able to talk about comparative assessments, even though this may be based on opinion rather than hard fact. Ask them about how they might bench-mark your organization's performance against their knowledge of what other organizations do, or how they do it. For example, one board member asked the audit partner about her view of their risk appetite: *'We assess our appetite for risk as a 6 on a scale of 1 to 10. Where would you assess us in comparison with other organizations?'* The board were surprised to be told that, in comparison, the audit team would assess them as a 9 out of 10, much less risk averse than the average for the sector. The board had to triangulate this information, but it prompted a useful reflection on their risk profile as a result.

Case study: Asking the right questions

When the financial controller of a medium-size electronics business resigned suddenly, there was understandable concern inside the organization. Finance department staff felt uncertain, and, as the news broke, local suppliers got in touch to express their concerns.

Senior management initiated a full review of key financial processes and although they found nothing serious, some recommendations from the previous external audit had not been implemented. There was also evidence that some members of staff had not been allowed to attend their scheduled professional training. This suggested a lack of attention to basic departmental disciplines and a failure of leadership.

In a later meeting, the audit partner told the board that he and his team had always had concerns about the financial controller's performance. He commented: *'We always thought that he was less able than you thought he was'.* The board, understandably, wondered why these concerns had not been voiced earlier. *'Why didn't you tell us this before?'* they asked. *'Because you didn't ask'* was the answer.

Summary

- When the board commissions work from any external adviser, they should be clear about three dimensions: what outcome the board wants from this piece of work, what they will do with the results and who, precisely, is the client.
- In commissioning work, it helps to be clear about what the board is looking for: information, explanation, evaluation, confirmation or facilitation – or some combination of them.
- The board should shape the commission appropriately, at the right cost and to the right timescale, by setting out the questions it wants answered.
- It is good practice for the independent board members to have a private discussion with the external auditors at least annually.
- External advisers have experience of, and insights into, other organizations, so it is always worth asking about comparisons and developments in the sector.

Checklist: Questions for boards and for advisers

Questions for the board to ask themselves	
When commissioning work:	What is the outcome we are looking for – information, explanation, evaluation, confirmation or facilitation?
	What do we intend to do with the results of the work commissioned from external advisers?
	Who specifically is the client?
	What is the reporting line for this work – for example, is it to come directly to the board or to a member of the executive?
Questions to ask when reviewing the results of the work:	Did we get what we need from this work? If not, how can we get the outcome we need?

Questions for the board to ask themselves	
Questions to ask when reviewing the results of the work:	Are we satisfied that the analysis has penetrated to the heart of the issues or problems?
	Are there any alternatives to the recommendations made that the adviser has considered but rejected? If so, why?
	What do other organizations do in this area?
General questions to ask external advisers:	In comparison to other organizations in this sector, how would you assess our approach to this topic?
	Would you say we are more or less risk-averse than other organizations in our sector?
	Have you seen other organizations undertake this kind of work or project and with what result?
	What do you see as the biggest risks facing our organization or our sector?
	What else are you seeing in our sector that we should pay attention to?
	What else have you noticed in working with us that the board should know about?

About ethics:
A new boardroom focus

The organization's values and ethics have become an important topic for boards in the 21st century. The word ethos is derived from the Greek word *ethos*, which means 'way of living' and so encompasses *every* conversation or action. Board members play a leading role in establishing the cultural context for ethical behaviour and independent board members have a particular role as stewards of the ethical standards of an organization.

Ethical matters have not always been so explicit in boardroom agendas, so it is worth understanding why they are now so significant. Here, there is a framework for the board's conversations about ethics, to help you to see how an ethical approach might play out in practice (Figure 16.1) as well as some questions for reflection.

The new ethical focus

The new emphasis on ethical approaches in every sector has been driven by a set of interconnected factors.

First, public views have changed: there is a widespread public expectation that organizations in every sector should behave ethically and transparently, and should attend to the environmental, social and governance (ESG) implications of what they do. Stakeholders watch board behaviour in this area, in particular, and take a more activist stance in expressing their views.

Second, a number of governance scandals in various sectors have occurred, resulting from some form of unethical behaviour somewhere inside the organization. In the aftermath, legislators and regulators have sought to remedy the situation with a range of new requirements that must become part of the board's remit.

Third, boards now have a more central role in developing strategy, and are therefore directly involved in the trade-offs they feel are often required, between economic considerations and social factors, such as a concern for nature and the impact on their local communities. The very real challenge is to move beyond this 'either–or' approach into Mode C working, as described in *Conversation 2: About the board*, steering the organization purposefully to ensure positive outcomes in every aspect of their operation.

As the board's remit has broadened in these areas, so scrutiny of individual ethics and behaviour has increased, both inside and outside the boardroom. Board members are the guardians of the organization's values and are required to have high levels of personal integrity. Many organizations now have explicit codes of conduct, and there are sector-wide standards that board members must live up to. For example, anyone holding any kind of office in the public sector in the UK must comply with the Nolan Principles, and there are similar sets of guidelines for those who work or volunteer in the charity sector.[54]

Talking about ethics

The stewardship role for board members plays out in conversation, as well as action: the way the board talks about and deals with ethical issues will shape the culture of the organization as a whole. Culture is the context that makes people want to do or be something – and behaving ethically is a key requirement for all organizations.

These conversations tend to fall into three modes: those that are mandated by statute or regulation; those that are of strategic importance; and those that are mission critical. As Figure 16.1 illustrates, these are interconnected, with each vital layer building on the other.

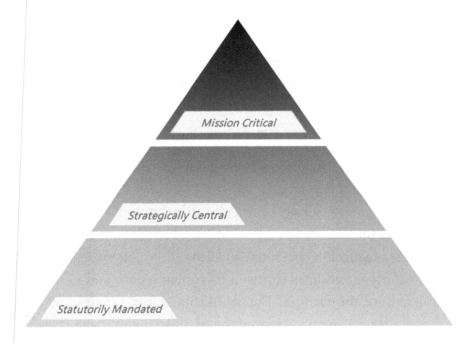

Figure 16.1   Talking about ethics

Layer 1: Statutorily mandated

The first layer of the model encompasses the laws, regulations, policies and procedures with which an organization must comply to be able to continue to operate. Board members will need to be assured about sustained compliance, which is no easy task. They will need to approve the relevant policies and ensure that the necessary infrastructure is in place to ensure compliance. This is an area of continuing attention, since new issues and concerns arise regularly, requiring discussion, sometimes difficult decisions and new measures to track progress.

At this level, the board is exercising managerial oversight, in Mode A working, as described in *Conversation 2: About the board*. Board members will want to talk with internal and external auditors as well as compliance staff to be sure they have sufficient resource. They will also want to explore the implications of new legislation and regulatory requirements, to be sure that they are properly understood and can be complied with.

The board's leadership in this layer of the framework ensures that externally imposed compliance requirements are built into its operational processes and that these are appropriate and sufficient.

Layer 2: Strategically central

Here, the board needs a broader conversation: to talk about how the organization's ethical approach will shape the way it operates. When that approach is strategically central, it will be built into key plans and policies, and into the statement of values, which are a foundation for the way the organization operates. It will also be visible everywhere: set out on the organization's website, in its annual report, and in recruitment literature, for example. The board should explicitly lead on this, so that the ethical approach becomes part of the culture of the organization.

The layers in this ethical framework are additive: the board will want to be assured that there is adequate audit and compliance capability, as in layer 1. But ethical considerations will appear in many discussions and decisions. For example, charity boards will want to debate investment policies for their endowment, particularly where a more ethical decision generates a different financial return. Universities now need to carry out more stringent due diligence on a donor before accepting a major donation. Because these issues are both central and difficult, some organizations have established ethics committees to guide them.

Many boards now focus on ESG considerations, which are becoming more strategically significant. These conversations have a wide focus: how the organization manages relationships with employees, suppliers and customers, as well as internal matters of governance and operational controls. They generate a range of specific initiatives, but may some-times look like managerial 'hobbies', or unconnected voluntary activi-ties that have no link to the organization's strategy. For example, there are choices in what kind of *pro bono* work might be offered – either simply resource to help to paint a community centre, or an offer of genuine expertise, such as supporting students from disadvantaged backgrounds into professional employment.

The board should talk about whether the organization has a planned and coherent approach to all these central ethical issues. And they will also want to see links between layer 1 compliance outcomes and organizational learning. For example, in some organizations, the compliance function and the HR team work closely together on devel-opment activities, not just to support compliance requirements, but to develop and embed the organization's ethical approach.

Layer 3: Mission critical

When the organization's ethical approach is mission critical, the board's conversations are different again. The focus is not simply to ensure that the organization's current business is carried out in a more ethical manner, but rather to put ethical *change* at the heart of every-thing it does. Increasingly, boards will have to grapple with this as a central part of their role.

This is visible in organizations with clear statements of purpose, which set out the social or environmental problem they are trying to solve. If such a purpose drives everything they do, the board's conver-sations about strategy will also be about mission-critical ethical issues, not just those inside the organization but also in society and the world.

These conversations have a broad scope, and a long-term focus, but they are not always easy. Board members will ask themselves diffi-cult questions about their understanding of the problems that they are trying to address and find no simple answers. And they bring dilemmas: the need to attend to purpose *as well as* performance, in exactly the same way in which they must balance the needs of the shareholder, who expects a return, with the needs of a wider group of stakeholders.

The increasing profile of the B Corporation Movement helps here, providing a framework and impetus for these vital ethical conversations. One example of this approach is in the work of B Lab UK, *'the non-profit network transforming the global economy to benefit all people, communities and the planet'.* Their aim is to *'redefine the role of business within our economic system so that every business is a force for good'.*[55] The driving motivation is the belief that the *'most challenging problems cannot be solved by governments and non-profits alone'.* The movement aims to harness the power of business by setting new standards for social and environmental performance, transparency and accountability. Organizations who reach these standards are certified as 'B Corporations' or 'B-Corps' – and there are already over half a million B Corps across the world. One example is Cook, the online supplier of frozen food, which describes its approach thus: *'From the founding of COOK in 1997, the ambition for the business was about more than money. Our goal was always to create a company that was good for shareholders while also Nourishing Relationships with everyone who comes into contact with it – employees, communities, suppliers and customers'.*[56]

New ethical issues

Having these conversations regularly at every layer is vital because the context is volatile and new ethical issues arise as a result. For example, regulators in many sectors recognize the importance of leadership and culture in organizations and are looking for ways to evaluate it and regulate it. This presents new challenges for regulators and for leaders.

Take a second example: new developments in technology such as artificial intelligence (AI), chatbots and systems such as ChatGPT (a natural language processing tool driven by AI technology) generate ethical questions. Is it ethical for an AI system to compose and send the response to an angry customer? If some of the organization's regulated activities are being performed by such software, decisions may no longer be verifiable, or repeatable, because of the learning built into the software, which changes what it does on each occasion. And it will be harder to ensure that the decisions made are unbiased and consistent with the organization's values. These ethical issues complicate the process of exploring the use of such new technology.

The increasing complexity of boardroom issues and their interconnectedness makes ethical issues harder to address, so these boardroom conversations are more necessary than ever before.

Ethics in practice: An example

The organization's ethical approach must translate into practice, into the way it deals with specific issues when they arise: one such issue is whistle-blowing. This policy allows a member of staff to raise a concern about danger or illegality that affects others, providing specific information to the employer or to a regulator. The disclosure may be about the alleged wrongful conduct of an employer, a colleague, client, or any third party. Examples of the situations covered include financial malpractice, criminal offences, risks to health and safety, failure to comply with a legal obligation, a miscarriage of justice or environmental damage. In many situations, the whistle-blower is not directly or personally affected by the danger or illegality, although they may be.

A clear and robust whistle-blowing policy is essential in an organization, and it must be supported by the board and clearly communicated to staff. Many boards will nominate a specific independent board member to be responsible for overseeing that the policy is effective. If a whistle-blowing concern is raised, the board will want to know that the agreed approach is being taken, that the individual who raised the concern suffers no detriment and that the issue raised is addressed properly and promptly.

The board may also wish to be assured that the culture of the organization is one where challenge and robust discussion are welcomed, and staff feel it is safe to speak out, so that concerns can be raised informally and immediately if necessary. Board members contribute to creating this culture in meetings with members of staff, as discussed in *Conversation 12: With staff*, and in the way they model the organization's ethical approach.

Case study: Understanding corporate responsibility

In 2020, allegations were raised that staff at a supplier for Boohoo plc, the fashion manufacturer, were being paid less than the minimum wage. This caused serious issues with investors and damaged the share price.

In response, the board commissioned an independent investigation, which found that the company had failed to appreciate its statutory requirements in respect of its suppliers, and, after a period of rapid growth, failed to face up to the obligations of an organization of its size.

The organization accepted the findings and developed a comprehensive plan to address the issues and to make a significant change to the way the company operated. The board also appointed Lord Leveson, a retired English judge, to provide independent oversight of its implementation. In his fifth and final report, he concluded that:

'*BooHoo had failed to appreciate that running a great company required social responsibility as well as growth. That message has been heard, understood and is in the course of being remedied, with very substantial steps already taken to recognise the wider picture beyond commercial success*'.[57]

Summary

- The way the board talks about and deals with ethical issues will shape the culture of the organization as a whole.
- This conversation offers a framework for the board's conversations about ethics: about statutory and mandatory issues, those which are strategically central to the specific organization and those which are mission-critical.
- The changing context raises new ethical issues regularly and the board must talk about them.
- The ethical approach must translate into practice, and be explicitly led by board members.

Checklist: Questions for reflection

Questions for reflection	
Layer 1: Statutorily mandated	Are our statements and policies compliant? How do we know?
	Does the organization have sufficient resource for compliance work?
	How does the board's oversight of compliance work?
Layer 2: Strategically central	How does the board set the ethical tone for the organization?
	How does the organization's purpose and strategy link to its policies?
	How do we monitor whether we have an ethical culture?
	Are our ESG activities planned and resourced properly and driven by an ESG strategy?
Layer 3: Mission critical	Do the measures we use link to the statement of purpose and to the organization's values?
	How do we ensure that our organization is not simply 'green washing'?

| Overall reflections | How does the organization view its ethical position – as a part of what we do, central to the way the organization works? |
| | How often do we talk about the ethical issues of new developments inside or outside the organization? |

About risk:
Preventing board blindness

Here, this book takes a different approach to the important subject of risk: it is not focused on topics such as enterprise risk management or third lines of defence, but instead is about how the behaviour of board members can place the organization at risk – and the conversations that need to take place to mitigate these risks.

Boards are complex social systems with their own power structures and affiliations – so-called 'soft governance'.[58] When you and your colleagues enter the boardroom, you are working within that context. If you observe the conversations, you may notice a number of behaviours that have significant implications for the board and the organization.

These are human phenomena, caused by a range of understandable feelings which everyone experiences – for example, fear of conflict, the wish to avoid damaging the group's unity, or the need for feedback and recognition. Because they are a function of being human, they can be intractable. They are also dangerous, because they may blind you to the critical risks that the organization faces and reduce your ability to see ways to mitigate or remove such risks.

The first action to take is to observe these phenomena clearly, as an ethnographer would do. Described in the following section are six psycho-social situations that can affect the way board members interact; the descriptions draw on psychological research and there are also several examples to illustrate the boardroom impact.

Addressing these behaviours is hard because the collective dynamic of the board can actually cause some of them. But, equally, boardroom conversations can also help to overcome them, or reduce their effect, as discussed below.[59]

Six risky behaviours and what to do about them

These six phenomena explain why people in groups behave in ways that they would never do individually, and why they may miss information and evidence that is in plain sight. When commentators have asked after the latest scandal '*Where was the board?*', the answer is '*They were there all the time – but they had gone blind*'.

Social loafing

Social loafing is a phenomenon where people put less effort into a group task, because they come to believe their individual efforts will have no impact and will go unnoticed – in other words, that there is no 'identifiability' of their contribution.[60]

Individual board members may not start out wanting to do a sub-optimal job – many will take up their role filled with enthusiasm, looking forward to having an impact by drawing on their experience. But, as set out in *Conversation 2: About the board*, although they join as individuals, they need to perform their task collectively – they may therefore see no results from their personal efforts, derive only low personal satisfaction from the task and start to feel that the task itself is not important. They may also start to feel that others may be better qualified for the task, which further reduces their desire to contribute.

This will be visible in the boardroom. Several chairs interviewed for this book expressed frustration that some board members did not appear to read the papers ahead of board meetings, while others did not contribute to discussions. In most boards, there are individuals who tend to contribute more than others, with some who regularly fail to take part in activities outside board meetings. This uneven engagement makes the group as a whole less effective.

The conversation

If there is an 'outbreak of social loafing', a board effectiveness review provides the space for a frank conversation about the reasons why people are less than fully engaged. For example, board members may not have been prepared for some of the more mundane aspects of boardroom life: in heavily regulated businesses, there may be an unexpectedly high workload in policy development, which comes as a surprise to those used to operating in less regulated organizations. Alternatively, it may be an issue of poor induction and a resulting lack of confidence. It may be because of information overload: there is nothing more likely to induce loafing than a three-inch thick board pack, most of which does not get discussed. It could be that too much is coming to the board, rather than to committees which could do the work more efficiently. It may simply be a level of disenchantment with the reality of the role, as one interviewee reported: 'I was used to operating in a fast-paced financial services organization, with frequent mergers and acquisitions activity. When I joined this government board, the job seemed to consist of endless papers for information and boring departmental visits. I felt I wasn't using my skills and my role on the board was simply window dressing!'

Establishing the cause is key to addressing the situation. Possible solutions may lie in changes to board agendas, to papers (*Conversation 8: About holding to account* has some ideas that may help), or with more effective chairing, covered in *Conversation 3: About chairing*. But if the board member thinks that the role is about 'turning up and voting yes' – perhaps someone who chose governance as opposed to golf for their semi-retirement – the chair needs to address this as a performance issue.

Conformity

Groups can have a powerful influence on individuals, even to the extent of changing views on things they know to be true. This phenomenon was first identified by Asch, whose experiments concluded that the social pressure of a group could result in an individual conforming to the beliefs of the group.[61]

There are two types of conformity:

- **normative conformity** – when an individual revises what he or she claims to believe, in order to go along with the group, but privately believes something different;
- **informational conformity** – when an individual actually revises their own privately held belief.

These two arise for slightly different reasons: the key factor in normative conformity is that the individual wants to be accepted by the group, whereas informational conformity occurs when individuals are looking to improve their own judgement by relying on people whom they believe have better judgement than they do.

Research indicates that people are more susceptible to the pressure of conformity in four particular circumstances, all of which are very common in boardrooms:

1. when the situation is unclear and ambiguous;
2. when the group around them is highly competent, credible and high status;
3. depending on how qualified the person feels;
4. the larger the membership of the group.

This behaviour reduces the board's ability to gain from its diverse experience, particularly in dealing with complex or ambiguous matters that require judgement. It may be visible when new members join a well-established board or where some members have particularly strong social links with others.

The conversation

Here, as in many such situations, the role of the chair is key in ensuring that a range of voices are heard and that ideas are fully explored. The key action is to ensure that a prevailing view is not established too early in the discussion. Encouraging people to be 'devil's advocate' may be a helpful way of generating an atmosphere of constructive dissent. Some chairs consciously choose not to express their own views on a topic at the outset of a discussion to avoid this phenomenon, and there is more about this in *Conversation 3: About chairing*. A good induction process helps new members to develop their own views. As relationships round the boardroom table develop, and mutual understanding increases, it becomes easier for the group to talk about different perspectives.

Pluralistic ignorance

Pluralistic ignorance occurs when various members of the group hold opinions but don't express them, believing (incorrectly) that they are inconsistent with the others in the group.[62] In these situations, people overestimate the extent to which their views differ from the group norm and remain silent. This behaviour may then become a norm, resulting in a spiral of silence round the boardroom table. This can get worse if those who are unwilling to express their different views are marginalized and become even less willing to speak up as a result.

In the boardroom, the lack of willingness to express individual views can do real damage. For example, the phenomenon of 'strategic persistence' may be a result of pluralistic ignorance – a situation where the organization continues to do something ineffective because everyone feels that everyone else is supportive. The key is to notice the behaviour, as this example illustrates.

Two medium-sized financial services organizations were in the final stages of a merger. On the face of it, this looked like a good proposition, since both organizations had a similar market position, culture and approach. When the IT director was brought in to the boardroom to give his view about systems capacity, he asked the board why it made sense to merge two such similar organizations – in his view, the combination would destroy value, rather than increase it. He commented, *'one plus one looks to me like less than two'*.

Startled by this question, the board realized that they had collectively pursued this strategy because they each believed other members of the board were keen to proceed – and that to object would look as if they were trying to protect their own position and the status quo.

The conversation

The chair's role is to encourage board members to contribute their different views, allowing the interrogation and testing of ideas. Some chairs, for example, make a point of speaking to each board member individually before the meeting to create the space for a free exchange of views. This prior understanding allows them to orchestrate a conversation in the board meeting where dissent is acknowledged as part of a constructive conversation.

Shared information bias

The point of having different skill sets on the board is for everyone to pool their collective knowledge and expertise so that this full range is available to the rest of the board. However, research suggests that groups spend much of their time examining information that is already shared between them, rather than seeking to surface information known only to a few of the board. This can sometimes be known as the 'hidden profile' effect.

Because people have access to shared information, they tend to focus on that information and the collective conversation is heavily influenced by it. This is known as a 'shared information bias' and it can make a group feel that they are usefully racing towards a consensus. In the boardroom, this behaviour can narrow any discussion about the strategy for the future, because the group is less likely to look for new or unfamiliar information or insights.

The conversation

Boards need new information and different perspectives in their discussions and *Conversation 7: About the future* sets out some ways to ensure that this becomes a regular part of the board's routine. This might involve board briefings from external advisers or allocating one particular board member to play a role as a 'devil's advocate' to test the strategy by deliberately introducing new ideas. Even making sure that there is sufficient time for a wide-ranging discussion of key strategic matters will help.

Groupthink

When the pressure for agreement prevents board members from looking at alternatives, groupthink is operating. This too is a function of social pressure and the desire to avoid confrontation. If dissenters remain silent too long – perhaps because they don't trust their own views – the pressure not to disrupt the growing sense of unanimity increases. This then generates a vicious circle, where it becomes harder and harder to express a contrary view.

Research shows that groups are more vulnerable to groupthink if they are:

- strongly led, with a leader who directs the agenda and limits the discussion;
- often required to make a decision quickly;
- cohesive, enhanced by the homogeneity of social background, or similar experiences, with high levels of affiliation;
- isolated from outside information and analysis.[63]

Such groups tend to be confident about their abilities and will generally be insulated from alternative ideas perhaps by pressure of workload and time. That pressure may also cause the group to look down on others with different opinions, perhaps even stereotyping other groups.

These characteristics describe many boards. Indeed, some of these qualities may actually help the board to be more effective at times – for example, a board with a strong chair who can focus discussion and help the board to respond quickly to urgent matters. But the risk of groupthink is considerable. For example, the board of a group of companies was discussing how to implement a series of strategies across four subsidiary companies. The CEO proposed a rapid roll-out programme, at some cost and risk, because *'the subsidiary organizations do not really understand what is required and are fighting a rear-guard action to oppose the change, so we need to get on with it'*. One independent board member noted the mocking and negative stereotyping of leaders in these subsidiaries and felt uneasy, because this was offered as the sole reason for the speed of the implementation project – and there was no opportunity to discuss any alternative approach.

The conversation

If you are on a board with a well-established team, here are some questions for reflection and then for collective discussion to help you to avoid groupthink.

- When was the last time there was any serious dissent in your discussions?
- What plans do you have to bring diverse views and experiences onto the board?
- How do you talk about other groups, both inside and outside the organization?

- How will you hear different perspectives or is most of the information brought to the boardroom by the CEO?
- Does the chair set an expectation that issues will be debated or challenged?
- What training does the board receive in order to understand issues in more depth?
- Do you know each other well enough to disagree – or too well for real discussion of differences of view?

There are other steps that boards can take, such as bringing in outside experts regularly, or allocating individual board members to keep a watching brief on new developments in the sector. The chair has a significant influence on this (*Conversation 3: About chairing*) and it is a topic for the board's own effectiveness review, too.

Group polarization

One particular form of groupthink is polarization.[64] When individuals in a group come together, it might be expected that the final outcome would be a compromise between their different positions. However, research shows that if their respective views are mostly risk-averse, the final consensus will be even more risk-averse. Conversely, if board members have a higher individual appetite for risk-taking, the final consensus is likely to be an even more risky conclusion.

This effect is known as group polarization, because of the tendency for groups to reach collective decisions that are more extreme than the group members would make individually. Their discussion and collective sharing of views tends to move decisions to the extremities of the range of views, because humans unconsciously seek a positive self-image in relation to others – one that is distinct and different.

This can affect decisions in the boardroom, particularly if they have to be made under pressure. Too rapid a decision-making process, too much emotion in the decision or no opportunity to reflect on it, can precipitate the organization engaging in inappropriate activity.

The conversation

A self-reflective board, aware of this phenomenon, might call for a pause in the meeting, or for a second look at a key decision at a later meeting, when board members have had a chance to reflect. Sometimes, taking a matter off-line for a series of individual conversations introduces delay, but makes for a better decision.

Summary

- Boards are complex social systems with their own power structures and affiliations – so-called 'soft governance'.
- There are six particular psycho-social situations that explain why people behave in groups in ways that they would never do individually and why they may miss information and evidence that was in plain sight.
  - *Social loafing* sees people putting in less effort when working as a group because they believe their individual efforts will not be identified and will have no impact.
  - *Conformity* describes the social pressure that can make individuals change their minds, or say that they have done so, when they have privately believed something different or have persuaded themselves that they were wrong in the first instance.
  - *Pluralistic ignorance* occurs when individuals incorrectly believe that their views are inconsistent with others in the group, and so remain silent.
  - *Shared information bias* happens when a group spends time rehearsing information that everyone has, rather than

looking for the new or unshared information that some members may have.

- ◻ *Groupthink* is a function of the social pressure and a desire to avoid confrontation, generating a vicious circle of surface unanimity, in which it becomes harder and harder to express a different view.
- ◻ *Group polarization* is a form of groupthink, in which the tendency is for the consensus to be a more extreme view, rather than a middle-ground compromise.
- Avoiding these risky behaviours requires a combination of open conversations, individual insight, excellent chairing, sound board schedules and diverse boards.

Checklist: Questions for reflection

Questions for reflection
Do we observe any of these behaviours in the boardroom?
Reflecting on my own behaviour: are there some occasions when I find myself 'socially loafing' and, if so, why?
Are there process changes that might help the board to reduce the risk of these behaviours – such as allowing sufficient time for discussion, agreeing to take some decisions off-line or allocating someone to take the 'devil's advocate' role?
Does the chair manage the meeting agenda and its dynamics to help the board to avoid these behaviours?

About a crisis:
When things go wrong

A crisis can have a huge impact on any organization, however well managed, and despite the best governance efforts of the board. Research conducted before the COVID-19 pandemic suggested that companies may experience some kind of crisis every four or five years.[65] But during the pandemic, every board experienced some form of crisis and board members are now more alert as a result.

Crises never arrive in the form you envisaged or planned for and you never get a second chance to avert them. The most effective responses are usually a blend of preparation and forethought, and they build on the levels of trust in the board, which allow rapid response in the moment. The kind of conversations the board has in a crisis can make a significant difference to the outcome. But those discussions will be much more effective if you have also talked in advance about the kinds of situations that you might face and how you would respond.

Conversations *before* something happens are as vital as those that happen *during* a crisis, but the conversations *afterwards* should not be missed in order to reflect on the lessons learnt in readiness for next time.

Before

Risks and 'red flags'

The board's discussions about key organizational risks lay the groundwork for any response to a crisis. Some risks may materialize as a single critical incident, which can be managed and may even have been planned for. Boards may already be watching for the 'red flags' that are regularly raised in the life of most organizations – decisions that bring additional risk because there is less understanding of them and less control over them.

Taken singly, critical incidents may be manageable, but in combination they may precipitate a crisis, if the board's governance arrangements are not strong enough – and they have done so in some situations. At the end of this Conversation, there is a generic list of 'red flags' to pay particular attention to.

Planning

Preparing for what might happen is always worth the effort, even though your plans almost never match what actually happens. Board conversations about risk should feed into business continuity planning, which the board should oversee. Board members may be involved in occasional discussion exercises to test these plans and how they would work in various hypothetical scenarios. Even if they are not directly involved, the board will want assurance that these plans are realistic and could be implemented quickly if something happens.

Ask whether those plans have been developed internally, or whether external agencies, such as the local fire service or the police, have been involved. To take one example: a 2013 fire in the data centre of a major UK utility was quickly extinguished, but the damage from the water that was used was greater than the damage from the fire itself. The organization could have anticipated this, and prepared a plan with the fire service to use foam only when firefighting in this particular building.

During

Assessing the situation

When something happens, the board needs to talk: is this a single, significant potential problem that could be managed, or is the combination of circumstances already spiralling out of control? For example, localized flooding of an office is a critical incident, but implementing the business continuity plan should be able to contain its effects.

Crises arise suddenly, are severe or large-scale, and typically come in three forms.

1. The sudden 'bolt from the blue' that will affect your organization specifically, such as an accident or the death of a key person;
2. A major failure of service, which may have been building up over time, but reaches a tipping point when it can no longer be controlled;
3. World events affecting many organizations, which are completely out of your control.

They are characterized by complexity: there will be a combination of factors that make it hard to see a solution, or even what is the right step to take.

The board should decide in conversation what kind of situation they are facing, because that will alter the way they react. Specifically, is the crisis caused by something that is suddenly going wrong, or by something where there has been wrong-doing? Is this, in other words, a genuine accident (type 1) or the outcome of poor behaviour over time (type 2)?

Key to this is the kind of information the board receives about the situation: is it sufficiently wide-ranging and triangulated from more than one source? Or is the board relying solely on its own collective assessment – believing its own propaganda? And one of the hardest conversations to have is with the CEO, to understand whether that person is culpable or visibly involved.

If the board doesn't understand the situation clearly, they may take action that makes the situation worse – for example, allowing the CEO to lead the response to a situation which that person has created, or allowed to happen.

Conversations in crisis

When a crisis occurs, the board and the organization are catapulted out of a relatively steady-state into chaos. These are abnormal circumstances: the pace increases, the emotional temperature goes up, and, although available data may increase, their reliability does not because the situation is usually so fluid.

In that situation, many boards start to function completely differently, with every board member running towards the problem, wanting to be involved in every conversation about what is happening and what should be done. This can be like a football team of 5-year-olds, where every player wants to get the ball, and score the goal.

To be effective, the board now needs to build on the strong working relationships that have been built in normal circumstances, through their conversations. Board members need clear roles and guidance about what to do and what not to do. A central organizing figure will take charge, usually the CEO or most senior leader, to lead the organization's response – and the board must understand this division of responsibilities from the first moment of the crisis. Board members will be kept informed, usually, but not necessarily, through the chair, but will not have time to debate issues or approve every action.

Rapid reactions

Board conversations need to be focused on two tasks: an assessment of the implications for the organization, and some immediate public statement, especially if there have been fatalities or injuries, to express authentic and appropriate reactions. Organizations can be slow to respond, while they debate internally, and this leaves a gap which will be filled by someone else's narrative. So clear messages need to be communicated quickly and in the right way, usually with no time for the board's detailed scrutiny.

As the crisis unfolds, the style of the board's conversations must change, with more listening and absorbing than talking. The CEO needs to provide frequent, succinct updates, making clear to the board which items are for information and which are for urgent decision. Much time is wasted on crisis calls discussing actions that have already been taken, because board members have struggled to understand long briefing papers. In a crisis, the clear and simple bullet point should be the rule for any papers and the conversations need to be correspondingly concise.

Talking with and listening to stakeholders

A key part of an effective response to a crisis is the connection with stakeholders. The chair of the board needs to organize board members, each 'marking' particular stakeholders to keep them informed, to let them know what is happening and when more information will be available. For example, one board member might be the key contact for the staff union, or for a particular supplier, while another is in discussion with the regulator. Conversations with stakeholders in this situation will be easier if there is a pre-existing relationship. This underlines the importance of regular stakeholder engagement, as set out in *Conversation 13: With stakeholders*.

If board members can listen as well as talk, they will learn how that stakeholder sees the unfolding events. That valuable information needs to be relayed as concisely as possible back to the organization – hence the need to prioritize conversations inside the organization around key issues of the moment.

Responding as a board

Crises demand much from board members: independent board members will need to consider themselves on duty most of the time, rather than waiting for the monthly rhythm of board meetings and briefings. They need to be up to date, reading everything they are sent immediately, since there is no time to play catch-up. They need to be in receive mode, rather than transmit mode, most of the time: listening to the latest development from inside the organization and to the reactions of stakeholders.

At the same time, however, the basic business of the organization and the board needs to continue, even during the crisis. Although board members may be devoting time to conversations with stakeholders and with each other, normal governance must continue to function at a time when it is more critical than ever.

The ripple effect

In heightened times of crisis, every communication to any one stakeholder will find its way out to all the others, not necessarily accurately, so these ripple effects have to be managed too. This seems to be a characteristic of these situations, rather than an indication that the communication is not being done well, so board members will need to work with this situation rather than resist it. This will never be easy to manage: for example, social media provides a mouthpiece for a wide range of reactions and views to be expressed, sometimes encouraging members of the public to take their own actions in response to the crisis.

Taking action

One useful guideline for organizations in crisis is to develop a set of actions increasing in significance, but to implement them one at a time and in sequence. If the organization reacts to the crisis by taking the most extreme action in an effort to contain the situation, there is nowhere else to go as the situation continues to develop. For example, in a contained crisis in one area, the senior department head will be expected to respond; then at the point where customers or service users need to be informed, the CEO may need to be visibly involved, with the chair of the board ready to step in if the situation escalates further.

Afterwards

Looking ahead

At some point, the board needs to start to look beyond the immediate and speculate in conversation how this might play out. Could there be, for example, a second wave or a further complication? And what actions does the organization need to take in the medium term in response to the current crisis or to prevent a future crisis?

This is where the board's conversation needs to switch back into medium and longer term thinking, considering how their future plans may have changed as a result of what has happened. A board that has rushed towards the problem must remember to step back when the situation is calmer.

Conversations about lessons from the crisis

Reflecting on the crisis, and talking about what went well and what should be done differently in future, is obviously valuable. Yet, few boards and organizations seem to find the time for this conversation. They miss the opportunity to draw out the lessons learnt, and to build them back into improved business continuity plans and into their own governance.

Case study: The value of strong working relationships

In the hours after a fire broke out at a UK care home for the elderly, the CEO and the chair worked in parallel on the response. The CEO focused on residents and staff, and specific stakeholders such as the fire service, insurers and local councils to make the necessary arrangements. The chair dealt with external communication, making sure that the organization was able to make its own announcements, rather than simply reacting to requests from the press. Rapid responses were vital, so there was often not enough time to co-ordinate closely. The strong working relationship between the chair and the CEO was a vital part of making this work, with an appropriate level of trust between the two compensating for the lack of detailed schedules and preparation time.

Summary

- Crises never arrive in the form that the board has planned for, but will affect the organization, however well-managed it is.
- *Before* the event, board members need to watch for the 'red flags' that may signal an approaching critical event, which may turn into a crisis, and plan ahead with business continuity plans.
- *During* the crisis, boards need to understand what they are facing: a sudden 'bolt from the blue', a failure of service, or a major world event.
- The board needs clear structures and rapid reactions to assess the impact and communicate appropriately. Board members will be on duty constantly, including attending to regular governance.

- Crises change the nature of board conversations: more listening than talking, more conversations with key stakeholders and concise reporting.
- *Afterwards*, the board needs to return to considering the medium and long term, as well as talking about the lessons learnt from the crisis.

Checklist: Generic 'red flags' to watch for

Factors which could *in combination* precipitate a crisis or prevent the board from noticing it:

Generic 'red flags' to watch for
An international joint venture with a new partner organization.
A new remote operation – the further away, the greater the risk.
A long-serving CEO or chair, or both.
Tactical, unconsidered diversification, moving away from the core business.
Excessive focus on winning awards or accreditation.
The distraction of new ideas and possible developments dominating discussion.
Unbalanced skills round the table – a lack of expertise in key areas, particularly finance, or of understanding of the basic business model of the organization.
A decision to outsource a key operational function with no previous experience of outsourcing.
Ritualized risk management processes, with insufficient attention to the real risks facing the organization.

Final words

Conversations with yourself: Reflecting as a professional practice

This book has been written to help people who want to be a member of a board that makes a difference. They want to understand what makes an effective contribution. But there is no recipe for this – no standard approach that will ensure you are adding maximum value – because being a board member is a complicated role, in a complex and rapidly changing context.

So, you have some choices about how you perform your role. The book offers suggestions, ideas, frameworks and occasionally even advice, to use in crucial conversations with others. Such interactions have always been a vital part of the shared work of the board, but now more than ever.

But the conversations with *yourself* are just as important. They will give you the space to think about your role as a board member. They will help you to get off the 'governance train-tracks', where the board goes through the same routines at every meeting, rather than responding to what is actually happening.

Reflecting on your own practice is necessary, precisely because your role will be unique to your situation. You will need to devise your own approach to it, given what you have to offer and what the organization needs from you. That's why this book contains a number of questions for reflection: to underline the importance of reflecting on your own practice – what you do in the boardroom and outside – in order to make your contribution more valuable.

Reflective practice as a disciplined approach for professionals is grounded on the work of Donald Schön.[66] It falls into two phases: reflection IN action, during the experience or event; and reflection ON action, afterwards. The first fuels the choice of how to act in the moment, while the second allows you to examine what happened, consider the effect of your choice and see if there were other options that might have been more effective. Obviously, it's the link between the two that matters – so that next time, you have more choices as you decide how to act.

And it's an iterative process, a continuous loop of experiencing something, reflecting on it and then taking a different action as a result. And then repeating that cycle. This is not in any sense self-indulgent navel-gazing, but the engine that drives better interactions.

It is a particularly important process now because the context for boardroom governance is shifting significantly. Most boards have a wider remit than they did 10 years ago. Whether you are a trustee, a governor, a director of a plc or serving on an advisory board in government, expectations have increased, as has the workload. Oversight of delivery of results to the shareholder now needs to be blended with attention to the needs of all the organization's stakeholders. Boards need to be focused both on organizational performance, but also on articulating their purpose and enacting it. Short-term pressures may have increased, but the board must also be focused on the long-term sustainability and contribution to society. And independent board members often need to be performance coaches as well as performance monitors.

This is why conversation with others and reflective conversations with yourself are key ingredients in making sense of the changing context and working effectively within it. Understanding complexity requires a range of different viewpoints, because no one person can see the situation in its entirety. Diversity of experience and expertise helps hugely, but only if it's shared – and that's where conversation is so vital: to exchange views, to increase understanding, to include a range of voices. These are not merely conversational niceties, but the foundations of good governance.

The very last words in this book are intended to encourage – literally, meaning to make brave. There will be a time in your board career when you need to speak out, to go against the crowd, to dig your heels in. This is not a comfortable place to be, but it may be the right thing to do.

Your board colleagues may lack the courage to back an idea – it's rare to be blamed for missing an opportunity. Perhaps nobody else has seen the risk you have spotted, or it may be that what really matters is not being talked about at all. This will be difficult, conversations may be confrontational, and you will feel out of step, but many governance failures are precipitated by someone in this situation who said nothing.

The ideas and insights in this book will help you to have the right conversations in the right way so that the board you serve on has the benefit of your experience and expertise. So that it can be the *heart* of the organization – central, vital, pumping the life blood of purposeful and proper activity – rather than the *appendix*, serving no obvious purpose but capable of killing you if it doesn't function properly.

List of figures

List of tables

Appendix:
Sources of useful information

Here, you will find a brief summary of the sources of information that may be of use to you in finding and applying for an independent board member role, and developing your skills once you have done so. This is not an exhaustive list of possible sources, and it has a UK focus, but it serves as a curated set of places to start your research.

Obtaining an independent board role

Some board roles will be advertised in the usual sources, but many involve search consultants, and some advertise roles on their websites. The names to look for include the 'Big 5' international executive search firms (Korn Ferry, Russell Reynolds, Spencer Stuart, Heidrick & Struggles and Egon Zehnder) as well as organizations such as Odgers Berndtson, GatenbySanderson or Veredus – and there are many others.

In the UK, public-sector roles are advertised on the 'Public Appointments' websites, which are specific to each nation in the UK. If you are looking for a role on a public board, there may well be similar arrangements in other countries.

Increasingly, both candidates and organizations use platforms to help to match boards with potential board members – combining head-hunting and technology. Many organizations use LinkedIn, while other platforms are membership organizations, offering listings of roles that are available. Some are invitation-only platforms, which conduct searches for employers, but will also allow potential applicants to upload their CVs.

Some are focused in particular areas, such as the Diversity Dashboard, which partners with UK organizations looking to increase the diversity of their boards.

Some sources combine recruitment with advice and support, particularly national or international network organizations. In the UK, these include organizations such as Women on Boards. Here, there are also some specific schemes to prepare people for public roles, such as The NExT Director Scheme, designed to develop and support the next generation of NHS board members in England.

Building your expertise

There is a wide variety of freely available resources to help build your knowledge and expertise.

Websites such as Board Agenda bring together news, analysis and expert comment about topics relevant to boards. Many of the search firms also have expert comment and useful blogs on their websites.

In addition to their public websites, some professional services firms also have invitational 'academies' which offer development and networking activities, and a range of development programmes for aspiring, new and experienced board members.

Other organizations offer development programmes on a fee basis – in the UK, examples include the Institute of Directors, the FT Board Director Programme and the Whitehall and Industry Group.

There are also professional associations that are sources of insight and development. Some span all sectors, such as the Chartered Institute of Personnel and Development (CIPD) in the UK, or the Institute of Chartered Accountants in England and Wales (ICAEW) or the Chartered Governance Institute.

Some are sector specific, such as the National Governance Association, which is the membership organization for governors, trustees and clerks of state schools in England. The other nations of the UK have similar sources – for example, Governors Cymru in Wales. The

Association of Governing Bodies of Independent Schools (AGBIS) is a source of support and guidance for the governors of independent schools.

Finally, regulatory bodies often offer a wide range of guidance and help for specific sectors, both what is required of the board as well as for assistance in specific situations. For example, in the UK, the Charity Commission provides a range of '5-minute guides' for charity trustees, while guidance for those serving on public boards is available on the UK government website.

Notes

1 See Roberts, McNulty and Stiles (2005). This was commissioned as a contribution to the Higgs Review, established under the chairmanship of Derek Higgs in 2002. The study examined the role and effectiveness of non-executive directors in the UK and made recommendations for a revised Combined Code, which has since been replaced by the UK Corporate Governance Code.

2 Based on Johnson (2018, p.129).

3 See Tett (2021).

4 Adapted from Gilmore (2016, p.14).

5 See Scott (2014).

6 See Argyris and Schön (1974).

7 See Scott (2014, pp.280–281).

8 See Starr (2016, p.60).

9 See Starr (2016, p.60).

10 This example comes from the work of Sir John Whitmore, one of the founders of the performance coaching industry. His 2009 book, *Coaching for performance*, is regarded as the founding text of the coaching profession.

11 See Scott (2014).

12 See Fama and Jensen (1983).

13 See Jensen and Meckling (1976).

14 See Clarke (1998).

15 See Davis, Schoorman and Donaldson (1997).

16 Arrangements for boards will vary by sector and geography: for example, in the UK, private-sector members of a unitary board will normally be elected

by shareholders, who also have the power to remove them, whereas in the public sector, board membership normally comes through an appointment process both for executives and non-executives. The role of the board may differ too: for example, a supervisory board will approve the accounts, might represent the organization to shareholders but may also have powers to intervene more directly if the interests of the organization are being affected by the actions of the management board.

[17] See the UK Corporate Governance Code (2018) www.frc.org.uk (accessed 8 March 2023) and Charity Governance Code (2020) www.charitygovernancecode.org (accessed 8 March 2023).

[18] See Review of Corporate Governance Reporting (2022) www.frc.org.uk (accessed 8 March 2023).

[19] See www.annual-report-triodos.com/2020/our-group/our-purpose-the-conscious-use-of-money

[20] See Garratt (2010, p.19).

[21] See Deloitte (2020, p.10).

[22] See Brennan (2022).

[23] In his book, Garratt (2010, ch.10) describes the board as a group of highly skilled individuals who come together occasionally, noting that although their responsibilities are 24/7, their interactions are intermittent.

[24] See Spencer Stuart (2017, ch.7). See also the UK Corporate Governance Code (2018) at: www.frc.org.uk/getattachment/88bd8c45-50ea-4841-95b0-d2f4f48069a2/2018-UK-Corporate-Governance-Code-FINAL.pdf

[25] See, for example, ICSA Guidance Note on the induction of directors (www.icsa.org.uk/assets/files/pdfs/guidance/030214.pdf) or the Charity Trustee Welcome Pack (www.gov.uk/government/publications/charity-trustee-welcome-pack/charity-trustee-welcome-pack#get-to-know-your-charity).

[26] See Financial Reporting Council (2020b). Principle B of the 2018 UK Corporate Governance Code states that, 'the board should establish the company's purpose, values, and strategy, and satisfy itself that these and its culture are aligned. Around half of our sampled FTSE 100 companies provided purpose statements. However, the quality of these varied greatly. There was a

tendency to conflate mission and vision with purpose; normally, mission and vision rely on a company's purpose to provide the reasons behind their goals. Too many companies substituted what appeared to be a slogan or marketing line for their purpose or restricted it to achieving shareholder returns and profit. This approach is not acceptable for the 2018 Code. Reporting in these ways suggests that many companies have not fully considered purpose and its importance in relation to culture and strategy, nor have they sufficiently considered the views of stakeholders in their purpose statements'.

[27] The Financial Reporting Council Guidance on Board Effectiveness (2018, Point 13) states: 'a sound understanding at board level of how value is created over time is key in steering strategies and business models towards a sustainable future… not limited to the value that is found in financial statements… [but includes] intangible sources of value are developed, managed and sustained – for example a highly trained workforce, intellectual property or brand recognition – is increasingly relevant to an understanding of the company's performance and the impact of its activity…'.

[28] You can find out more at www.gov.uk by searching the publications for Companies House Strategy from 2020 onwards.

[29] See the guide produced by the Special Interest Group of the Institute of Risk Management (2018).

[30] See Nolin (2016). This is a conclusion from the research undertaken by Judith Glaser (2016) for her book *Conversational intelligence*.

[31] Nassim Nicholas Taleb (2008) used this term to describe random financial events in his book *Fooled by randomness*.

[32] This diagram is based on the three horizons model described by Bill Sharpe and Tony Hodgson (2006).

[33] Paul Schoemaker, quoted in Augier and Teece (2018, pp.1–9).

[34] Paul Schoemaker, quoted in Villanueva (2021).

[35] See Roberts, McNulty and Stiles (2005).

[36] See Dunne (2021, p.235).

[37] The Financial Reporting Council's culture report (2021, Section 11b) underlines the importance of alignment: 'Best practice suggests that boards should seek periodic assurance that underlying policies and practices, as well as promoted behaviours, are in line with corporate purpose, values and strategy'.

[38] See Parker et al. (2020).

[39] See Financial Reporting Council (2018).

[40] See Neate (2017).

[41] Various regulatory regimes in the UK set out such requirements, as for example, the UK Financial Reporting Council in their guidance on board effectiveness, the National Governance Association in their advice on governing board self-evaluation questions for schools, and principle 5 of the Charity Code.

[42] Interview, CEO of the UK Financial Reporting Council, November 2022.

[43] National Audit Office (2009).

[44] See Royal Holloway, University of London, and Involvement and Participation Association (2021).

[45] The UK-based Chartered Institute of Personnel and Development (CIPD) website sets out some best practice and a range of ideas on this topic. See the Bibliography.

[46] See Freeman (2010).

[47] See Freeman and By (2022).

[48] See Charity Governance Code Steering Group (2017).

[49] See Committee of University Chairs (2020).

[50] See Spencer Stuart (2021).

[51] See Martin (2019).

[52] See Steelyard (2019).

[53] See Financial Conduct Authority (2019),

54 For the Nolan Principles, go to www.gov.uk/government/publications/the-7-principles-of-public-life/the-7-principles-of-public-life--2 (accessed 19 June 2023). For charity ethical principles, go to www.ncvo.org.uk/help-and-guidance/running-a-charity/charity-ethical-principles/#/ (accessed 19 June 2023).

55 For more on B Lab, go to www.bcorporation.net/en-us/ (accessed 19 June 2023).

56 For more on Cook, visit www.cookfood.net/info/bcorp/ (accessed 19 June 2023).

57 For more on this, see www.marketscreener.com/quote/stock/BOOHOO-GROUP-PLC-16023307/news/boohoo-Sir-brian-Leveson-s-final-report-to-the-Board-39692399/ (accessed 19 June 2023).

58 See Thuraisingham and Healy (2019).

59 For more information, see Merchant and Pick (2010).

60 See the description of the Ringelmann effect in Ingham et al. (1974).

61 See Asch (1955).

62 Read more about pluralistic ignorance in Westphal and Bednar (2005).

63 Janis (2008) analyses groupthink.

64 The polarization phenomenon is discussed in Myers and Lamm (1976).

65 See *Financier Worldwide* (2017).

66 See Schön (1991).

Bibliography

Allcock Tyler, D. (2020). *It's a battle on the board.* Liverpool: Directory of Social Change.

Argyris, C. and Schön, D.A. (1974). *Theory in practice: Increasing professional effectiveness.* San Francisco: Jossey-Bass.

Asch, S.E. (1955). 'Opinions and social pressure', *Scientific American*, 193 (5), 31–35. DOI: https://doi.org/10.1038/scientificamerican1155-31.

Augier, M. and Teece, D.J. (eds) (2018). *The Palgrave encyclopedia of strategic management.* Basingstoke: Palgrave Macmillan.

B Lab (2022). *B Lab Global Site.* Available at: www.bcorporation.net/en-us/ (accessed 15 April 2023).

Brennan, N.M. (2022). 'Is a board of directors a team?', *The Irish Journal of Management*, 41 (1), 5–19. DOI: https://doi.org/10.2478/ijm-2022-0001.

Brown, G., Kakabadse, A. and Morais, F. (2020). *The independent director in society: Our current crisis of governance and what to do about it.* Basingstoke: Palgrave Macmillan.

Brown, G. and Peterson, R.S. (2022). *Disaster in the boardroom: Six dysfunctions everyone should understand.* Basingstoke: Palgrave Macmillan.

Cadbury, A. (2002). *Corporate governance and chairmanship: A personal view.* Oxford and New York: Oxford University Press.

Cavanagh, B. (2022). *Governing with purpose.* Northwich: Practical Inspiration Publishing.

Charan, R. (2005). *Boards that deliver: Advancing corporate governance from compliance to competitive advantage.* San Francisco: Jossey-Bass.

Charan, R., Carey, D.C. and Useem, M. (2014). *Boards that lead: When to take charge, when to partner, and when to stay out of the way.* Boston, MA: Harvard Business Review Press.

Charity Commission (2014). *How to report a serious incident in your charity.* Available at: www.gov.uk/guidance/how-to-report-a-serious-incident-in-your-charity (accessed 26 February 2023).

Charity Governance Code Steering Group (2017). *Charity Governance Code.* Available at: www.charitygovernancecode.org/en (accessed 8 June 2023).

Chartered Institute of Personnel and Development (2022). *Employee Voice | Factsheets | CIPD.* Available at: www.cipd.co.uk/knowledge/fundamentals/relations/communication/voice-factsheet (accessed 8 June 2023).

Clarke, T. (1998). 'The stakeholder corporation: A business philosophy for the information age', *Long Range Planning,* 31 (2), 182–194. DOI: https://doi.org/10.1016/s0024-6301(98)00002-8.

Committee of University Chairs (2020). *The Higher Education Code of Governance.* Available at: www.universitychairs.ac.uk/wp-content/uploads/2020/09/CUC-HE-Code-of-Governance-publication-final.pdf (accessed 8 June 2023).

Cossin, D. (2020). *High performance boards: A practical guide to improving and energizing your governance.* Chichester: Wiley.

Davey, L. (2019). *The good fight: Use productive conflict to get your team and organization back on track.* Vancouver, BC: Page Two Books.

Davis, J.H., Schoorman, F.D., and Donaldson, L. (1997). 'Toward a stewardship theory of management', *The Academy of Management Review*, 22 (1), 20–47. DOI: https://doi.org/10.2307/259223.

Deloitte (2020). *Chair of the future: Supporting the next generation of business leaders.* Available at: www2.deloitte.com/content/dam/Deloitte/uk/Documents/about-deloitte/deloitte-uk-chair-of-the-future.pdf (accessed 1 July 2022).

Deloitte (2022). 'Mind the purpose gap', *Deloitte Insights.* Available at: www2.deloitte.com/uk/en/insights/topics/strategy/mind-the-purpose-gap.html (accessed 8 June 2023).

Dunne, P. (2007). *Running board meetings: How to get the most from them.* London: Kogan Page.

Dunne, P. (2021). *Boards* (2nd edn). London: Governance Publishing and Information Services Ltd.

Dunne, P. and Morris, G.D. (2009). *Non-executive director's handbook.* Oxford: Elsevier.

Fama, E.F. and Jensen, M.C. (1983). 'Separation of ownership and control', *SSRN Electronic Journal*, 26 (2). DOI: https://doi.org/10.2139/ssrn.94034.

Financial Conduct Authority (2019). *Senior Managers and Certification Regime.* Available at: www.fca.org.uk/firms/senior-managers-certification-regime (accessed 22 January 2023).

Financial Reporting Council (2018). *Guidance on board effectiveness.* Available at: www.frc.org.uk/getattachment/61232f60-a338-471b-ba5a-bfed25219147/2018-Guidance-on-Board-Effectiveness-FINAL.PDF (accessed 8 June 2023).

Financial Reporting Council (2020a). *The UK Stewardship Code 2020.* Available at: www.frc.org.uk/getattachment/5aae591d-d9d3-4cf4-814a-d14e156a1d87/Stewardship-Code_Dec-19-Final-Corrected.pdf (accessed 8 June 2023).

Financial Reporting Council (2020b). *Annual review of the UK Corporate Governance Code.* Available at: www.frc.org.uk/getattachment/53799a2d-824e-4e15-9325-33eb6a30f063/Annual-Review-of-the-UK-Corporate-Governance-Code (accessed 8 June 2023).

Financial Reporting Council (2021). *Creating positive culture: Opportunities and challenges.* Available at: www.frc.org.uk/getattachment/9fc6c466-dbd2-4326-b864-c2a1fc8dc8b6/FRC-Creating-Positive-Culture-Report_December-2021.pdf (accessed 8 June 2023).

Financier Worldwide (2017). 'The role of the board in crisis scenarios'. Available at: www.financierworldwide.com/the-role-of-the-board-in-crisis-scenarios#.Yv4UzXbMI2w (accessed 15 April 2023).

Freeman, E. and By, R.T. (2022). 'Stakeholder capitalism and implications for how we think about leadership', *Journal of Change Management*, 22 (1), 1–7. DOI: https://doi.org/10.1080/14697017.2022.2037184.

Freeman, R.E. (2010). *Strategic management: A stakeholder approach.* Cambridge: Cambridge University Press.

Freeman, R.E., Martin, K., and Parmar, B. (2007). 'Stakeholder capitalism', *Journal of Business Ethics*, 74 (4), 303–314. DOI: https://doi.org/10.1007/s10551-007-9517-y.

Gardner, H. and Peterson, R. (2019). 'Back channels in the boardroom: How to prevent side conversations between directors from blocking progress', *Harvard Business Review*. Available at: https://hbr.org/2019/09/back-channels-in-the-boardroom (accessed 5 January 2023).

Garratt, B. (2010). *The fish rots from the head. The crisis in our board-rooms: Developing the crucial skills of the competent director*. London: Profile.

Gevurtz, F. (2004). 'The historical and political origins of the corporate board of directors.' Available at: https://scholarlycommons.law. hofstra.edu/cgi/viewcontent.cgi?article=2341&context=hlr (accessed 23 March 2023).

Gilmore, J.H. (2016). *Look: A practical guide for improving your observational skills*. Austin, TX: Greenleaf Book Group.

Glaser, J.E. (2016). *Conversational intelligence: How great leaders build trust and get extraordinary results*. Brookline, MA: Bibliomotion Inc.

gov.uk (2018). *Charity trustee welcome pack*. Available at: www. gov.uk/government/publications/charity-trustee-welcome-pack/ charity-trustee-welcome-pack#get-to-know-your-charity (accessed 27 February 2023).

Hall, E.T. (1959). *The silent language*. New York: John Wiley & Sons.

Hemus, J. (2020). *Crisis proof*. Brighton: Rethink Press.

Ingham, A.G., Levinger, G., Graves, J., and Peckham, V. (1974). 'The Ringelmann effect: Studies of group size and group performance', *Journal of Experimental Social Psychology*, 10 (4), 371–384. DOI: https://doi.org/10.1016/0022-1031(74)90033-x.

Institute of Risk Management (2018). *Horizon scanning: A practitioner's guide*. Produced by the Innovation Special Interest Group of the Institute of Risk Management. Available at: www.theirm.org/media/7423/ horizon-scanning_final2-1.pdf (accessed 8 June 2023).

Isaacs, W. (1999). *Dialogue and the art of thinking together: A pioneering approach to communicating in business and in life*. New York: Currency.

Isaacs, W. (2017). *Conversations that change the world.* Available at: www.strategy-business.com/article/Conversations-That-Change-the-World (accessed 10 June 2022).

Janis, I. (2008). 'Groupthink', *IEEE Engineering Management Review,* 36 (1), 36. DOI: https://doi.org/10.1109/emr.2008.4490137.

Jensen, M.C. and Meckling, W.H. (1976). 'Theory of the firm: Managerial behavior, agency costs, and ownership structure', *Journal of Financial Economics,* 3 (4), 305–360.

Johnson, G. (2018). *Fundamentals of strategy* (4th edn). Harlow: Pearson Education.

Laffin, S. (2021). *Behind closed doors. The boardroom: How to get in, get on, and make a difference.* Southampton: FCM Publishing.

Legislation.gov.uk. (2016). *Companies Act 2006.* Available at: www.legislation.gov.uk/ukpga/2006/46/section/172/2011-04-22 (accessed 8 June 2023).

MarketScreener (2022). *Boohoo: Sir Brian Leveson's final report to the board.* Available at: www.marketscreener.com/quote/stock/BOOHOO-GROUP-PLC-16023307/news/boohoo-Sir-brian-Leveson-s-final-report-to-the-Board-39692399/ (accessed 15 April 2023).

Martin, D. (2019). *Union vote of no confidence in DMU leadership.* Available at: www.leicestermercury.co.uk/news/leicester-news/unions-vote-no-confidence-de-2545853 (accessed 14 April 2023).

Merchant, K.A. and Pick, K. (2010). *Blind spots, biases and other pathologies in the boardroom.* New York: Business Expert Press.

Moyo, D. (2021). *How boards work.* London: Bridge Street Press.

Myers, D.G. and Lamm, H. (1976). 'The group polarization phenomenon', *Psychological Bulletin,* 83 (4), 602–627. DOI: https://doi.org/10.1037/0033-2909.83.4.602.

National Audit Office (2009). *Board evaluation questionnaire.* Available at: www.nao.org.uk/insights/board-evaluation-questionnaire-4/ (accessed 14 April 2023).

National Audit Office (2017). *Regulation: A short guide to.* Available at: www.nao.org.uk/wp-content/uploads/2017/09/A-Short-Guide-to-Regulation.pdf (accessed 8 June 2023).

National Council for Voluntary Organisations (2022). *Charity ethical principles.* Available at: www.ncvo.org.uk/help-and-guidance/running-a-charity/charity-ethical-principles/#/ (accessed 15 April 2023).

National Governance Association (2014). *Governing board self-evaluation questions.* Available at: www.nga.org.uk/Knowledge-Centre/Good-governance/Effective-governance/Governing-Board-Self-Review-(1)/Self-evaluation-questions.aspx (accessed 8 June 2023).

Neate, R. (2017). 'Persimmon chair quits over failure to rein in CEO's "obscene" £100m+ bonus', *The Guardian*, 15 December. Available at: www.theguardian.com/business/2017/dec/15/persimmon-chair-resigns-chief-executive-obscene-bonus (accessed 8 June 2023).

Nolin, W. (2016). 'Three practices to ease difficult conversations', *Medium.* Available at: https://medium.com/@wendynolin/3-practices-to-ease-difficult-conversations-33c7e1fc14ae (accessed 14 April 2023).

Parker, J. (2017). *A report into the ethnic diversity of UK boards.* Available at: https://assets.ey.com/content/dam/ey-sites/ey-com/en_uk/news/2020/02/ey-parker-review-2017-report-final.pdf (accessed 8 June 2023).

Parker, J., Atewologun, D., Bhandari, S., Mahy, H., Sir, C., Olisa, K., Trevor, O., ... and Cover, O. (2020). *Ethnic diversity enriching business leadership: An update report from The Parker Review.* Available at: https://assets.ey.com/content/dam/ey-sites/ey-com/en_uk/

news/2020/02/ey-parker-review-2020-report-final.pdf (accessed 8 June 2023).

Patterson, K., Grenny, J., Switzler, A., and Macmillan, R. (2012). *Crucial conversations: Tools for talking when the stakes are high.* New York: McGraw-Hill.

Roberts, J., McNulty, T., and Stiles, P. (2005). 'Beyond agency conceptions of the work of the non-executive director: Creating accountability in the boardroom', *British Journal of Management,* 16 (S1), S5–S26. DOI: https://doi.org/10.1111/j.1467-8551.2005.00444.x.

Royal Holloway, University of London, and Involvement and Participation Association (2021). *Workforce engagement and the UK Corporate Governance Code: A review of company reporting and practice.* Available at: www.frc.org.uk/getattachment/56bdd5ed-3b2d-4a6f-a62b-979910a90a10/FRC-Workforce-Engagement-Report_May-2021.pdf (accessed June 8 2023).

Schön, D.A. (1991). *The reflective practitioner: How professionals think in action.* Aldershot: Ashgate.

Scott, S. (2014). *Fierce conversations: Achieving success at work and in life one conversation at a time.* New York: Berkley Books.

Sharpe, B. and Hodgson, T. (2006). *Intelligent infrastructure futures technology forward look: Towards a cyber-urban ecology.* Available at: https://assets.publishing.service.gov.uk/government/uploads/system/uploads/attachment_data/file/300337/06-520-intelligent-infrastructure-technology.pdf (accessed 8 June 2023).

Spencer Stuart (2017). *Boardroom best practice.* Available at: www.spencerstuart.com/research-and-insight/boardroom-best-practice (accessed 17 December 2022).

Spencer Stuart (2021). *Stakeholder voices in the boardroom*. Available at: www.spencerstuart.com/research-and-insight/stakeholder-voices-in-the-boardroom (accessed 8 June 2023).

Starr, J. (2016). *The coaching manual: The definitive guide to the process, principles and skills of personal coaching* (4th edn). Harlow: Pearson Education.

Steelyard, L. (2019). 'DMU admits "governance inadequate" after inquiry by regulator'. Available at: www.leicestermercury.co.uk/news/de-montfort-university-admits-governance-3040738 (accessed 14 April 2023).

Taleb, N.N. (2008). *Fooled by randomness: The hidden role of chance in life and in the markets*. New York: Random House.

Taylor, B.E., Ryan, W.P., and Chait, R.P. (2005). *Governance as leadership: Reframing the work of nonprofit boards*. Hoboken, NJ: Wiley.

Tett, G. (2021). *Anthro-vision: A new way to see in business and life*. New York: Avid Reader Press.

Thuraisingham, M. (2021). *Identity, power and influence in the boardroom*. Abingdon and New York: Routledge.

Thuraisingham, M. and Healy, J. (2019). *Identity, power and influence in the boardroom: Actionable strategies for developing high impact directors and boards*. Abingdon and New York: Routledge.

Turkle, S. (2015). *Reclaiming conversation: The power of talk in a digital age*. New York: Penguin Books.

Veenman, D. and Cannon, D. (2014). 'The strategic importance of conversations', *Developing Leaders: Executive Education in Practice*, 15, 28–34.

Villanueva, J. (2021). 'Boards, scenario planning and digital transformation', *Forbes*, 8 February. Available at: www.forbes.com/sites/julianvillanueva/2021/02/08/boards-scenario-planning-and-digital-transformation/?sh=6a6742b055ab (accessed 11 March 2023).

Webb, C. (2016). *How to have a good day: Harnessing the power of behavioral science to transform our working lives*. New York: Crown Business.

Westphal, J.D. and Bednar, M.K. (2005). 'Pluralistic ignorance in corporate boards and firms' strategic persistence in response to low firm performance'. *Administrative Science Quarterly*, 50 (2), 262–298. DOI: https://doi.org/10.2189/asqu.2005.50.2.262.

Whitmore, J. (2009). *Coaching for performance: The principles and practice of coaching and leadership* (4th edn). London: Nicholas Brealey Publishing.

Wilson, P. (2022). 'The art of leaving a trustee role well', *Getting on Board*. Available at: www.gettingonboard.org/post/the-art-of-leaving-a-trustee-role-well (accessed 26 February 2023).

Zeldin, T. (2000). *Conversation*. Mahwah, NJ: Hiddenspring.

Acknowledgements

There are many people we want to thank because their ideas, stories and insights have gone into the material in this book and have helped us to write it. Some we have interviewed as part of the research for the book; others are those we have learned from while working with them over the years, on boards in various organizations and sectors. We are deeply grateful to you all, and particularly to: Dyfed Alsop; Professor Marcus Alexander; Steve Brandon; Ranila Ravi Burslem; George Elkington; Henry Elkington; Rob Fraser; Matt Greenfield; Jonathan Hutchings; Alison Johns; Tracey Killen; David Richards; Colin Skellett; Matthew Smith; Emma Taylor; Sir Jon Thompson; Robert Walther; Bevis Watts and Professor Steven West.

We have also benefited from invaluable advice and help during the process of turning an idea into a book ready for publication, so we are also hugely grateful to: Alison Jones for her guidance, wisdom and encouragement, as well as the team at Practical Inspiration Publishing, especially Sandra Stafford for her thoughtful development editing; Mary McCormick and the team at Newgen Publishing UK, for their brilliant design work; and Mark Carden for his artistry and insight in creating the illustrations for this book.

Index

About the authors

Kathryn Bishop and Gillian Camm have each spent decades in boardrooms in private-sector companies, public bodies, charities, and schools, working with boards as Chair, Senior Independent Director, non-executive, or executive member. Their focus on making boards more effective blends this real-life practical experience with their research and teaching.

Kathryn is an Associate Fellow at the Saïd Business School at the University of Oxford, where she teaches and works with boards of global organizations. She combines her teaching with practical experience working in organizations. She has served on boards in England and Wales in the public, private and charity sectors, including as the first Chair of the Welsh Revenue Authority, set up to raise revenue in Wales for the first time in 800 years. Her first book, *Make Your Own Map*, about women's working lives, was published in 2021, and she received a CBE in the 2021 Birthday Honours list for services to diversity and public administration. Her website sets out her other publications and videos as well as her blog (www.kathryn-bishop.com).

Gillian runs her own executive coaching and consultancy business, drawing on her extensive experience on boards in the private and public sectors, including roles as the senior independent director at Wessex Water, a main board director at Clerical Medical Investment Group, and a world-wide partner of the Hay Group. She was a member of the General Medical Council (GMC) and the first lay Chair of the Fitness to Practise Committee. She has also served as Chair of the Leadership Foundation for Higher Education and as Chair of the Board of Governors of the University of the West of England. In these roles, she has been actively involved in working with investors, regulators and consumer groups, and in reviewing and re-developing systems of governance. For example, she led a review of governance of the GMC following the Shipman Inquiry and of university governance in Wales culminating in the publication of the Camm Review in 2019. She has also written for the *Journal of General Management* and the *Financial Times*.